"A hunt is clear, clean air, fragrant with balsam and spruce—the heat and the silence and the unbelievable color of the desert—the ghostly forms of the jingle-horses seen through frosty morning mist. . . . It is the circle around the campfire when men speak of the hunt and of elemental things."
—Rutherford G. Montgomery, High Country, 1938

Majestic
BIG GAME

From the Editors of Voyageur Press

Voyageur Press

Majestic
WILDLIFE
LIBRARY

Edited by Danielle J. Ibister
Designed by Kjerstin Moody
Printed in Hong Kong

First Hardcover Edition
00 01 02 03 04 5 4 3 2 1
First Paperback Edition
01 02 03 04 05 5 4 3 2 1

Library of Congress Cataloging-in-Publication Data
Majestic big game: the ultimate tribute to North America's greatest game animals / from the editors of Voyageur Press.
     p. cm. — (Majestic wildlife library)
     ISBN 0-89658-439-9
     ISBN 0-89658-539-5 (pbk.)
     1. Big game hunting—North America Anecdotes. 2. Big game animals—North America Anecdotes. I. Voyageur Press. II. Series.

    SK40.M275   2000
    799.2'6'097—dc21   99-14624
                     CIP

Distributed in Canada by Raincoast Books
9050 Shaughnessy Street
Vancouver, B.C. V6P 6E5

Published by Voyageur Press, Inc.
123 North Second Street
P.O. Box 338, Stillwater, MN 55082 U.S.A.
651-430-2210, fax 651-430-2211
books@voyageurpress.com
www.voyageurpress.com

Educators, fundraisers, premium and gift buyers, publicists, and marketing managers: Looking for creative products and new sales ideas? Voyageur Press books are available at special discounts when purchased in quantities, and special editions can be created to your specifications. For details contact the marketing department at 800-888-9653.

Permissions
We have made every effort to determine original sources and locate copyright holders of the excerpts in this book. Grateful acknowledgment is made to the writers, publishers, and agencies listed below for permission to reprint material copyrighted or controlled by them. Please bring to our attention any errors of fact, omission, or copyright.

"The Ultimate Bull" from *How I Got This Way* by Patrick F. McManus. Copyright © 1994 by Patrick F. McManus. Reprinted by permission of Henry Holt and Company, Inc.
"My First Mountain Sheep" by Jack O'Connor. Copyright © 1945 by Jack O'Connor.
Excerpt from *The Deer Pasture* by Rick Bass. Copyright © 1985 by Rick Bass. Reprinted by permission of Texas A&M University Press.
"Antelope Camp" by Tom Carpenter. Copyright © 1997 by Tom Carpenter. Reprinted by permission of the author.
"Caribou Dream" by John Barsness. Copyright © 2000 by John Barsness. Printed by permission of the author.
"A Bowhunting (Ob)session" by Bill Heavey. Copyright © 1998 by Bill Heavey. Reprinted by permission of the author.
"Ghost Bears" by J. B. Stearns. Copyright © 1997 by J. B. Stearns. Reprinted by permission of the author.
Excerpt from *Heart and Blood* by Richard Nelson. Copyright © 1997 by Richard Nelson. Reprinted by permission of Alfred A. Knopf, Inc.
"Little Benny's Rug" by Glenn Balch. Copyright © 1934 by Glenn Balch. Reprinted by permission of Olin Kendall Balch, Mary Birch, Nikki Balch Stilwell, and Betty Lou Weston.
"The Edges of an Elk Hunt" by Dave Hughes. Copyright © 1998 by Dave Hughes. Reprinted by permission of the author.

Page 1: *Caribou in a northern wilderness. (Photograph © Jeanne Drake)*
Pages 2–3, main photo: *An American elk. (Photograph © Du Van Smetana)*
Page 3, inset: *An Arizona hunter displays his pronghorn quarry. (Courtesy of the Arizona Historical Society/Tucson, #71908)*
Facing page: *Black bear crossing water on fallen tree. (Photograph © Bill McRae)*
Page 6: *Whitetail buck in velvet. (Photograph © Daniel J. Cox/Natural Exposures Inc.)*

CONTENTS

INTRODUCTION   9

Chapter 1
CHASING TROPHIES   13
The Chronicle of a Chromatic Bear Hunt by Rex Beach   15
The Ultimate Bull by Patrick F. McManus   35

Chapter 2
THE FIRST   43
My First Mountain Sheep by Jack O'Connor   45
Excerpt from The Deer Pasture *by Rick Bass*   57

Chapter 3
BIG GAME COUNTRY   71
Antelope Camp by Tom Carpenter   73
Caribou Dream by John Barsness   87

Chapter 4
TOILS OF THE HUNT   97
A Bowhunting (Ob)session by Bill Heavey   99
Ghost Bears by J. B. Stearns   107

Chapter 5
THE HUNTING EXPERIENCE   117
Excerpt from Heart and Blood *by Richard Nelson*   119
Little Benny's Rug by Glenn Balch   131
The Edges of an Elk Hunt by Dave Hughes   147

MAJESTIC BIG GAME

North American big game hunting: It is the bearskin rug, the mounted head with antlers or horns. Yet it is more than trophies. It is creeping through pre-dawn light to be ready for elk as the first rays of sun filter through the trees. It is climbing rocky slopes to reach the formidable heights where bighorn sheep and mountain goat reside. It is stifling the laughter that wells up at the clownish antics of a black bear. It is a noisy flight in a bush plane to be dropped in the heart of a wild and unspoiled Canadian wilderness to meet a caribou migration. It is crawling painstakingly slow across the dusty prairie to close in on a herd of pronghorn.

Big game hunting is the camaraderie of camp life, sitting around a fire in the twilight hours exchanging tales and good-natured gibes. It is the hearty meals of potatoes and onions and—hopefully—elk liver. It is discovering, in the morning, mule deer tracks, made in the middle of the night, no less than one hundred yards from the tent. Or grizzly tracks no less than five feet from the tent. It is the look of admiration—even envy—on the face of fellow hunters as a regal buck is packed into camp.

Big game hunting is also solitude. It is the silence of an October morning in a Pennsylvania woods, broken only by the chatter of squirrels and the crying of jays. It is long tramps, muffled by six inches of new snow, along mountainous trails. It is the hush that descends after a single thunderous bang of the rifle brings down the quarry.

A Rocky Mountain bighorn ram. (Photograph © John W. Herbst)

Big game hunting is an American tradition. It reaches back to the ancient native peoples of this nation who hunted big game for food and clothing, but also for prestige and trophies. It reaches back to the colonists who built their livelihoods around the natural resources of America, the resources that included big game animals. It reaches back to our grandparents' time, when big game were still abundant in the mountains and plains and forests.

Since then, big game hunting has changed. Permits are required, animals have retreated into more reclusive surroundings, the woods are peppered with blaze orange suits, and a daughter may accompany her father on a hunt. But the flavor of the meat, the trophy hung on the wall or spread out on the floor, these details remain, untainted by change—though perhaps a little seasoned by it.

Including time-honored essays by legendary writers such as Jack O'Connor and Rex Beach, plus contemporary stories by renowned outdoors authors Rick Bass and John Barsness, this anthology combines the classic with the fresh, the exotic with the commonplace. No matter when or where they were written and despite their varied aspects, these stories are hunting tales—timeless in their own right, because the essence of hunting will never change.

This book is a virtual extravaganza of North American hunting literature. Enjoy the stories of Rex Beach and Patrick McManus, who, in their own comical ways, attempt to bag a trophy. Relish the stories of Jack O'Connor and Rick Bass, in which first-time hunts become unforgettable experiences. Appreciate the particular joys of big game country, from "the prairie, windy solitude and pronghorns" in Tom Carpenter's tale to the Arctic world that John Barsness explores. Identify with the staunch mindset—and resulting exertion—that places Bill Heavey behind a bow day after day and J. B. Stearns in a Vermont woods with a cumbrous black bear. And, of course, love what makes the taking of game more than just a successful hunt, as elucidated in the stories of Richard Nelson, Glenn Balch, and Dave Hughes.

This anthology is not only a compilation of hunting stories, but it is also a collection of spectacular big game photography. An array of talented photographers contributed images for this book, including Robert E. Barber, Erwin and Peggy Bauer, Terry Berezan, Alan and Sandy Carey, Daniel J. Cox, Jeanne

Drake, Jeff Foott, Michael H. Francis, D. Robert Franz, Cary and Curt Given, John Herbst, Henry H. Holdsworth, Rich Kirchner, Stephen Kirkpatrick, Ann Littlejohn, Doug Locke, Thomas D. Mangelsen, Michael Mauro, Bill McRae, Gary McVicker, Mark and Jennifer Miller, Neal and Mary Jane Mishler, William H. Mullins, Stan Osolinski, Michael Peck and Dolores Fernandez, James Prout, Jeffrey Rich, Len Rue Jr., Bob Sisk, Dušan Smetana, Tom Tietz, Tom Walker, and Art Wolfe.

This book is a tribute to North America's big game animals, to the animals whose presence tempers our wilderness with majesty.

A herd of wapiti cross the snow-swept panorama of Wyoming elk country. (Photograph © Thomas D. Mangelsen/Images of Nature)

Chapter 1

CHASING TROPHIES

"You remembered elk bugling in the fall, the bull so close you could see his chest muscles swell as he lifted his head, and still not see his head in the thick timber; but hear that deep, high mounting whistle and the answer from across another valley. You thought of all the heads you had turned down and refused to shoot, and you were pleased about every one of them."
— Ernest Hemingway, "The Clark's Fork Valley, Wyoming," 1939

THE CHRONICLE OF A CHROMATIC BEAR HUNT

By Rex Beach

In ancient times, a trophy was often engraved with a dedication to a god or goddess. Following in ancient tradition in "The Chronicle of a Chromatic Bear Hunt," Rex Beach scours an Alaskan island for a trophy to dedicate to a goddess—that is, a trophy grizzly to bring home to his color conscious wife.

In 1897 at the age of 19, Beach was lured away from his studies at a Chicago law school by the discovery of gold along the Klondike River in Canada's Yukon. He lit out for the north country, where he "went broke—then flush—then broke again, time after time." Beach never reached the Klondike, but, during his travels, he read a volume of Jack London's short stories, adventurous tales much like the ones he lived daily. Inspired, he penned his own story and submitted it to *McClure's*; when it was promptly accepted for fifty dollars, Beach devoted himself full time to writing and became a regular contributor to *McClure's* and other outdoors magazines.

His first novel, *The Spoilers*, was a bestseller in 1906. He went on to write over thirty novels and plays, many of which were brought to the big screen. The following story was originally published in Beach's 1921 autobiographical book *Oh, Shoot! Confessions of An Agitated Sportsman*.

T he biography of the average big-game hunter is a bitter hard-luck story. As compared with his work, the twelve labors of Hercules were the initiatory stunts of a high-school sorority. If this were not so, we would have no game left. The "big-horn" and the Alaskan grizzly would soon be quite as extinct as the dodo.

When Fred Stone and I determined to go bear hunting we chose Alaska, for several reasons. First, it was farther away than any other place we knew of, and harder to get to than certain suburbs of Brooklyn. Secondly, there are lots of bears in Alaska—black, white, gray,

Pages 12-13, main photo: *An elk with an asymmetrical 6×4 rack. (Photograph © Thomas D. Mangelsen/ Images of Nature)*
Page 13, inset: *Wyoming hunters display their elk, bighorn, and bear trophies. (Courtesy Buffalo Bill Historical Center, Cody, WY)*
Facing page: *The grizzly bear, native to northwest North America, is considered a subspecies of the brown bear and has cousins on Alaska's Kodiak Island, as well as across Asia and in parts of Europe. (Photograph © Henry H. Holdsworth/Wild by Nature)*

blue, brown, and the combinations thereof; enough to match any kind of furniture or shade of carpet. And I had been kindly but firmly informed that my trip would not be considered a success at our house unless I brought back a mahogany-brown skin, shading to orange, for the living room, and a large pelt not too deeply tinged with ox-heart red, to match the dining room rug. Fred was told likewise that the boss of his bungalow would welcome bear rugs of a French-gray or moss-green tint only.

We began to hunt immediately upon leaving New York, and had secured some fine specimens before reaching Chicago, but we killed most of our bears between St. Paul and Billings, Montana.

It was while dashing through the Bad Lands that Fred suggested bear dogs. "Great!" said I. "They'll save us a lot of work and be fine company in camp." Accordingly, we wired ahead for "Best pair bear dogs state of Washington," and a few hours after our arrival at Seattle they came by express. They were a well-matched pair, yclept Jack and Jill, so the letter stated; both were wise in their generation and schooled in the ways of bear.

"They are a trifle fat," we read, "but they will be O. K. if you cut down their rations. Both are fine cold trailers. Kindly remit hundred dollars and feed only at night." We were informed that in Jill's veins coursed the best blue blood of Virginia, and that, although she was no puppy in point of years, her age and experience were assets impossible to estimate. This rendered me a bit doubtful, for Alaska is not a land for fat old ladies, but Fred destroyed my misgivings by saying:

"Take it from me, she's all right. We don't want any debutante dogs on this trip."

Jack was more my ideal. He had the ears of a bloodhound, the face of a mastiff, and the tail of a kangaroo, while his eyes were those of a tragedian, deep, soulful, and dark with romance. When he gave tongue, we decided he must have studied under Edouard de Reszke. . . .

For five days we plowed northward on a typical ratty Alaskan steamer, a thing of creaks and odors and vermin. On a drizzly May morning we docked at Cordova, the town which had sprung up at the terminus of Mr. Heney's railroad. The road was not really Mr. Heney's, but belonged to the Morgan-Guggenheim interests, being destined to haul copper from their mines two hundred miles inland. Mr. Heney was building it for them, however, and everybody looked upon it as his personal property. It was hours before breakfast time when we arrived, but "M. J." himself was at the dock, for a purser on one of his freight steamers had apparently mislaid a locomotive or a steam shovel or some such article which Mr. Heney wished to use that morning, and he had come down to find it. He was not annoyed—it takes something more than a lost, strayed, or stolen locomotive to annoy a man who builds railroads for fun rather than for money and chooses a new country in which to do it because it offers unusual obstacles.

He welcomed us, drippingly, with a smile of Irish descent which no humidity nor stress of fortune could affect.

"I'm sorry you didn't arrive yesterday," he said, "for it looks as if the fall rains had set in." It was the 21st of May and this was no joke, for Cordova is known as the wettest place in the world.

"Bear?" said Mr. Heney. "Yes, indeed. We'll see that you get all you want." And from that moment until we left Alaska with our legal limit of pelts he made us feel that the labors of his fifteen hundred men, the building of his railroad, and the disbursement of millions of dollars were, as compared with our comfort and our enjoyment, affairs of secondary importance. And when we described to him the tints of our wall paper and rugs we got the impression that, whether we needed bears lavender, bears mauve, or bears cerise, it was thenceforth a religion with him to see that we found them.

As to guides, there were no regular guides in this neighborhood, since there were no tourists—every resident had to earn his money honestly. But there were fellows about who knew the woods—Joe Ibach, for instance. He had just come in from a prospecting trip and might care to go a-bear hunting. So we descended upon Joe. Certainly he'd go. He didn't care to guide, however, as he had never "gid" any, but he'd show us a lot of bears, and carry the outfit, and row the boat, and do the cooking, and chop the wood, and build the fires, and perform the other labors of the camp. As for regular guiding, though, he guessed

This grizzly sports the silver-tipped "grizzled" fur that gave the subspecies its name. (Photograph © Gary A. McVicker)

we'd have to see to that ourselves until he learned how. When we spoke about wages, he said he didn't think that sort of thing was worth money, showing conclusively that he was not a real guide. He had a long, square jaw and a steady eye, which looked good to us, so we agreed to do the guiding if he would do the rest of the things he had mentioned—and see that we did not get lost. As to those mysterious glaciers towards which I had been working these two years, Mr. Heney said we could not reach them yet. The Copper River delta was full of rotten ice, and the banks were so choked with snow that it was impossible to take an outfit up before the slews cleared. Out at Camp Six, however, a number of bears had been seen, one in particular so large that no day laborer could look upon his tracks and retain a sense of direction. Only the section bosses could stand

their ground after one glance at his spoor.

We were installed at Camp Six by 5:30 on the following afternoon and had unchained our dogs. At 5:49 Jack had found a porcupine. A man came running to inform us that he was "all quilled up," and so he was; his nose, lips, tongue, and throat were white with the cruel spines.

"Get them out quick, or they'll work in," we were advised, and somebody produced a pair of tweezers, with which we fell to. But Jack suddenly developed the disposition of a wolf and the strength of a hippopotamus. Followed a rough-and-tumble which ended by our getting his shoulders to the mat on a "half Nelson" and hammer-lock hold. Those quills which we did not remove from the dog with the tweezers we pulled out of each other after the scrimmage.

At 6:15 Jill notified us plaintively that she had

discovered a brother to Jack's porcupine and had taken a bite at him. By the time we had pulled the barbs from her nose our supper was cold.

"Well, it's a good thing for them to get wised up early," Fred remarked, wiping the blood and sweat from his person. "They'll know enough not to tackle another porcupine. They're mighty intelligent dogs."

We were still eating—time, 6:44—when a voice outside the mess tent inquired, "Whose dog is that with his nose full of quills?"

We looked at each other and Joe commenced to laugh.

"Are there any dogs besides ours around this camp?" I inquired of the waiter.

"No, sir."

It was nearly midnight before Jill ran down her second victim and raised us from our slumbers by her yells, but by that time we had become so dexterous with the pincers that we could feed each other soup with them, so we were not long in getting back to bed.

The next day it rained. It rains every day in this country, but nobody minds it. In fact, the residents declare they don't like sunshiny weather, asserting that it cracks their feet. One Cordovan had undertaken to keep a record of the sunshine, on the summer previous, but had failed because he had no stopwatch.

Before setting out Fred called my attention to Joe's rifle.

"It looks like an air gun," said he. "It wouldn't kill a duck."

Joe yielded the weapon up cheerfully for examination, and it did indeed look like a toy. Its bore was the size of a lady's lead pencil, it was weather-beaten and rusty, and the stock looked as if it had been used to split kindling.

"She's kind of dirty now," the owner apologized, "but I'll set her out in the rain to-night, and that will clean her up."

My experience with Alaskan grizzlies has shown me that they are hard to kill and will carry much lead, hence in close quarters a bullet with great shocking power is more effective than one which is highly penetrative; but when we suggested adroitly to Joe that

he use one of our extra guns instead of this relic, he declined, on the ground that his old gun was easier to carry.

We splashed through miles of muskeg swamp toward the forest where the big bear had been seen. We sank to our knees at every step; low brush hindered us; in places the surface of the ground quaked like jelly. We were well into the thickets before the dogs gave tongue and were off, with us crashing after them through the brush, lunging through drifts, tripping, falling, sweating. For ten minutes we followed, until a violent din in the jungle ahead advised us that their quarry was at bay.

Joe took his obstacles in the manner of a stag, finally bursting through the brush ahead of us with his air gun in his hand, only to stop and begin to swear eloquently.

"What is it?" I yelled, hip deep in a snowdrift.

"Have you got them pinchers handy?" came his answer.

For five days we combed those thickets and scoured the mountain sides without a shot, for those educated bear dogs got lost the moment we were out of sight, and made such a racket that we were forced to take turns retrieving them. They were passionately addicted to porcupines. No sooner were they through with one than they tackled another, and when not wailing to be "unquilled" they "heeled" us, ready to climb up our backs at the appearance of any other form of animal life.

"If we saw a bear they'd run between our legs and trip us up," declared Joe, disgustedly.

Deciding, finally, that this section was too heavily timbered to hunt in without canine assistance, we sought more open country, and the next high tide found us scudding down the sound in a fast launch towards an island which for years had been shunned because of its ugly bears. Not a week before a party of native hunters had been chased into camp by a herd of grizzlies, hence we were in a hurry.

We skimmed past wooded shores which lifted upward to bleak snow fields veiled by ragged streamers of sea mist. Into a shallow, uncharted bay we felt our course, past cliffs white with millions of gulls, under towering columns of rock which thrust wicked

Grizzlies, like most bears, are omnivorous. Some 10 to 20 percent of an average grizzly's diet comes from meat, although coastal grizzlies may rely almost entirely on salmon for sustenance. (Photograph © Terry Berezan/Wilderness Images Ltd.)

This grizzly lives on the Alaska Range of Denali National Park. (Photograph © Robert E. Barber)

fangs up through a swirling ten-mile tide and burst into clouds of shrieking birds at our approach.

We anchored abreast of two tumble-down shacks, and, as the afternoon was young, prepared for exploration. Ahead of us, rolling hills rose to a bolder range which formed the backbone of the island. The timbered slopes were broken by meadows of brilliant green, floored, not with grass, but with oozy moss.

"We've got three guns in the party," said Joe, noting the preparations of Little, the owner of the launch, "so I'll take the camera instead of my rifle. If we see a bear, them dogs can't trip up more than two of us, which will leave one man to shoot and one man to use the machine."

For hours we tramped the likeliest-looking coun-try we had seen, but the wet moss showed no scars, the soft snow gave no evidence of having been trod, so I suggested that we divide, in order to cover more territory. Fred and Little, escorted by Jack and Jill, headed towards the flats, while Joe and I turned up-ward towards the heights.

Far above timber line we found our first sign, and farther on more tracks, all leading down the south-ern slope and not in the direction of our launch; so away we plodded, over crater lakes half hidden and choked with fifty feet of snow, skidding down crusted slopes, lowering ourselves hand over hand down gutters where the snow water drenched us from above. In time we left the deeper snows for thick brush, broken by open patches, and a ten-o'clock twilight was on us when we spied a fresh track. The moss had slipped and torn beneath the animal's weight, and the sharp slashes of the claws had not yet filled with seepage.

"He's close by," said Joe, shifting the camera. "Gee! I wish I'd brought my gun instead of this thrashing machine," and for the first time I realized that I had a new, small-calibered rifle with me, and had selected this day to try it, not expecting to have to rely upon it.

At a half run we followed down the trail, for there was no difficulty in picking it up wherever it crossed an open spot; but, without warning, the hillside ahead of us dropped off abruptly and we emerged upon the crest of a three-hundred-foot declivity choked with devil clubs and underbrush, the tops of the spruce showing beneath us. Joe altered his course towards the right when I saw, over the edge and not thirty feet away, a grizzled scruff of hair looking like the back of a porcupine.

"There he is!" I called, sharply. "Look out for yourself!"

I stepped to the edge of the bluff, for after my first glimpse that angry fur had disappeared—and looked down directly into the countenance of the largest grizzly in the world! Halted by our approach, he had paused just under the crest.

I have seen several Alaskan bears at close range, but I never saw one more distinctly than this, and I never saw a wickeder face than the one which glared up at me. His muzzle was as gray as a "whistler's" back, the silver hairs of his shoulders were on end like quills, while his little pig eyes were bloodshot and blazing.

"What luck!" I thought, wildly, as the rifle sights cuddled together, but in that fraction of a second before the finger crooks, out from the brush behind him scrambled another bear, a great, lean, high-quartered brute of cinnamon shade, appearing, to my startled eyes, to stand as tall as a heifer.

Now, I never happened to be quite so intimate with a pair of grizzlies before, and since that moment I have frequently wondered how they happened to impress me so strongly with the idea of a crowd. The woods seemed suddenly filled with bears, and involuntarily I swept the glades below to see if this were a procession, or a bear carnival of some sort. That instant's weakness cost me the finest pelt I ever saw, for at my movement bear number one leaped, and as I swung back to cover him I saw only a brown flank disappearing behind a barrier of projecting logs. At that distance I dared not take a chance on other than a head shot, so I jumped back, peering through the brush at our level, hoping to see him as he emerged.

Joe rushed forward to the edge of the hill, as if about to assault the cinnamon with his camera, and stepped directly between me and where I expected bear number one to show.

"Shoot! Shoot! Give it to him before he gets up here," he yelled, hoarsely.

"Get out of the way!" I shouted, with my eyes glued upon the vegetation at his back.

He was still screaming: "Shoot! Shoot!" when his voice rose to a squeak, for up through the under-growth lunged the big cinnamon, nearly trampling him. The bear rose to its hind legs and snorted, while Joe did a brisk dance, side-stepping neatly from underneath his photographic harness and fairly kicking himself up and out of his rubber boots. Before either footgear or camera had ended its flight he had sized up the dimensions of every spruce tree within a radius of forty rods, and was headed for the most promising.

I dare say my own movements were purely muscular at the time. I got out of Joe's way in time to avoid being badly trampled, only to glimpse through my sights a brown rump over which the brush was closing, and remember deciding that with five shots in an untried weapon I didn't care to chance a tail shot, especially with that other big gray bear concealed within forty feet—and more especially since Joe had staked the only available tree.

In the days which followed I cursed myself bitterly at the memory of those white-hot seconds.

"Gosh 'lmighty! If I'd only had a six-shooter!" panted Joe, regarding me with disgust. "Why didn't you give it to him?"

"I wanted to get the big one first," said I.

"The *big* one! You never saw a bear any bigger than *that* one, did you?"

"Yes; I tried to get a shot at the old gray one."

"Do you mean to say there was two of 'em?"

"I do! And the big one was in yonder all the time. He may be there now, for all I know."

As Joe picked up the camera he said, very quietly:

"I guess your eyesight was a little bit scattered.

Above: *Powerful swimmers, coastal grizzlies spend much of their time in the water. (Photograph © D. Robert Franz)*
Facing page: *This grizzly lives in Katmai National Park, home to the world's largest sockeye salmon run. The grizzlies of this region grow fat on the calorie-rich seafood and can weigh as much as 1,500 pounds. (Photograph © Art Wolfe)*

You 'ain't seen any bear for quite a spell, have you?"

I resented the innuendo, and began to declare myself vigorously, when he interrupted: "Come on! Let's get after them," and away we went up the mountain side, running until we were breathless, guided plainly by great patches of torn moss and heavy indentations. We ran upgrade until I stumbled and staggered from exhaustion; we ran until my legs gave out and my lungs burst; we ran until I feared I should die at the next knoll; and we kept on running until I feared I might not die at the next knoll. Up, up, and up we went, until, two hundred yards above, a moving spot amid the timber halted us.

"G-g-give it to him!" gasped Joe. But the sights danced so drunkenly before my eyes that it is a wonder I did not shoot myself in the foot or fatally wound my guide. Then we were off again across sink holes scummed over with rotten ice into which we broke, up heartbreaking slopes, and through drifts where we wallowed halfway to our waists. In time the tracks we followed were joined by others, at which Joe wheezed:

"By g-gosh! You—were—right; there was—two! Come on!"

But, having righted myself in his eyes, I petered out completely. My legs refused to propel me faster than a miserable walk, so I turned the gun over to him and he floundered away, while I flopped to my back in the center of a wet moss patch and hoped a bear would come and get me.

Ten minutes later I heard him empty the magazine, but as he reappeared I knew the shots had been long ones.

"Say! That old gray one made the brown feller look like a cub," said he, and we were miles away from the scene before he broke our silence to remark:

"You were wise not to shoot. If I'd 'a' known that big one was so close to me I'd 'a' tore my suspenders out by the roots and soared up over the treetops."

Stone and Little, having covered the flats unsuccessfully, were rowing into the mouth of the creek when we slid down the bluff above the launch, but at my recital of our adventure Fred went violently insane and was for setting out for the scene of our encounter at once. Eventually he was calmed and we rolled up for a few hours' rest on the floor of the launch.

I was half roused by the coffeepot sliding off the stove into my face. A few minutes later the ashpan emptied its contents over me, and I awoke under a bombardment of dishes, oil cans, and monkey wrenches, to find the boat on her beam ends in the mud, with every movable thing inside of her falling upon us. Little was swearing softly in his underclothes and bare feet.

"The tide is out and she's standing on her hands," he explained. "Confound a round-bottomed boat, anyhow!"

We stood on the starboard wall of the cabin to dress, then walked ashore where there had been eighteen feet of water on the night previous, to cook our breakfast in the rain.

Up the hills again we went, determined to see at last what was in those bear dogs of ours. For five miles we trailed our game, across snow fields where their tracks were knee-deep, over barren reaches where it took all our skill to pick up the signs, until, without warning, the dogs gave tongue and went abristle. They were off, with us after them, the woods ringing to their music, the bears just out of sight through the timber.

It was during the next hour that I proved to my own satisfaction that a two-hundred-pound man, considerably out of condition, can't outrun a bear. Perhaps it is because the bear knows the country better.

Half a mile after I had quit running I found Fred panting and dripping on the other side of a stream.

"Where's Joe?" I called.

The shades of a grizzly bear's coat range from blond to nearly black. This blond Alaskan grizzly is only one of the shades of "black, white, gray, blue, brown, and the combinations thereof" Beach describes in his tale. (Photograph © Len Rue Jr.)

"At the rate he was going when I lost sight of him, he'll be due in Nome about noon, if his boots hold out," Fred answered, sourly. "Where's Little?"

"Fallen by the wayside. How did you cross the creek?"

"I didn't! I ran through it. I'm wet to the ears."

"Those are nice bear dogs of ours," I ventured; at which my companion's remarks were of a character not to be chronicled.

"'Kindly remit hundred dollars and feed only at night,'" he quoted. "Say, if those laphounds ever crab another shot for me I'll—"

"And I'll do the same," I declared, heartily; and we shook hands over the compact.

We found Little at camp, clad in a pair of bath slippers, drying out his clothes, but Joe did not show up until nearly ten that night, and then he came alone.

"Did you kill those college bear dogs?" we inquired, hopefully.

"I couldn't get close enough," he said.

"Did you get a shot at the bears?"

"No! About twelve miles back yonder those two picked up five more. Your eighty pounds of *Mother Goose* dog had four tons of bear on the hike when I quit. It looks like they're heading toward the north side of the island, and if we take the launch around to Big Bay to-night we may be able to pick them up to-morrow."

It was high tide when Jack and Jill appeared on the bank, and as Joe boosted them over the rail they beamed upon us as if to say:

"This has indeed been a glorious day, and we'll make this bear hunt a success if it takes all summer." We forbore to saddle them with what lay upon our souls.

We anchored in Big Bay as a three-o'clock dawn crept over the southern range, only to be awakened a few hours later by another avalanche of pots and pans. The launch was doing her morning hand stand, and I found a streamlet of cylinder oil trickling down my neck. Fred had been assaulted from ambush by a sack of soft coal, while the cupboard had hurtled a week's grub into the midst of Little's dreams. Joe alone was unconscious of his bedfellows, which com-

prised the rest of our cargo; he was slumbering on his back, snoring like a sea lion at feeding time.

A mile of tide flats glistened between us and the shore; on every hand the hills were white with desolate snow. Having dressed stiffly, propped at various angles, we ate a cold breakfast, for the stove would not draw, and had it drawn we could not have held the coffeepot against it; then Joe and I lowered ourselves into the slime overside, for Little had decided to stay with the launch until high tide, while Fred's heels were blistered so that he could not wear his boots. We went without the dogs.

At nine that night I staggered wearily out from the timber on to the beach. A mile of mud lay between the bank and the water, and two miles beyond that I sighted the launch. Fred and Little heard my shots, and by the time I had reached the low-water line they were under way. Out another half mile into the creeping tide I waded, until it was up to the tops of my boots. I was utterly exhausted, my feet were bruised and pounded to a jelly, every muscle in me ached. For fourteen hours Joe and I had shoved ourselves through the snow, in places waist-deep, crossing cañons, creeping up endless slopes until we had traversed the island and the open sea lay before us. Snow, snow, snow everywhere, until our eyes had ached and our vision had grown distorted.

We had found the tracks of those seven bears, but they were miles away and headed toward the west, whither we could not follow. We had become separated later and I had come home alone, ten miles as the crow flies, across the most desolate region I ever saw.

I had followed a herd of five bears for several miles, but had abandoned the chase when it grew late. One track I measured repeatedly from heel to toe of the hind foot. It took my Winchester from the shoulder plate clear up two inches past the hammer.

Two hours after I was aboard we heard Joe's air gun popping faintly. He, too, had followed those five bear tracks, holding to them an hour after my trail had sheered off. We had covered better than thirty miles of impossible going and were half dead.

The next day found us back at the cabins; for the north side of the island was too killing, and as Little

Inland grizzlies often range 500 square miles to find sufficient food, while this coastal grizzly feeds on the abundant salmon of its home and probably ranges only about 10 square miles. (Photograph © Jeff Foott)

had business to attend to, he left us, promising to send the launch back in ten days. Then followed as heartbreaking a week as I ever endured. Every morning we were off early, to drag ourselves in ten, twelve, perhaps fourteen hours later, utterly exhausted. Every noon we stopped to dry out over a smoky fire, for an hour's work on the slopes threw us into a dripping perspiration, which the chill wind discovered at the first breathing spell.

Our feet were constantly wet from the melting snow, and the rain did what remained to be done. We stood barelegged and shivering in the snow, our feet on strips of bark, the while we scorched our underclothes and swore at the weather. Finally, on one particularly drenching morning, Fred and I struck and declared for rest. Our feet and ankles were so swollen that we hobbled painfully, while our systems yelled for sleep. . . .

Three days later, when Little sent back the launch, we were ready to quit in disgust and head towards the Copper River glaciers, for the bears seemed utterly to have forsaken this island. We could find no fresh signs, we could discover no indications as to where they were feeding.

A mile from the mouth of the bay we ran hard aground, and a falling tide left us high and dry, but held upright this time by the cabin doors, which we had removed and used as props.

"I'm going over into those woods where Little and I went the first day," Fred announced, and Joe went with him, while I, disheartened, went fishing in the channel.

Having drifted opposite the mouth of a tiny creek without a strike, I rowed ashore and wandered aimlessly back into the open flat through which the stream meandered. It was the first time since landing in Alaska that I had been without my gun, and within three hundred yards from the shore I encountered fresh bear tracks. As I regarded them, a movement at my back caused me to whirl, and there, where I could have hit him with a stone, was my bear observing me curiously.

We looked each other over for several moments. We were both blonds, although his fur was a bit lighter than mine. When I moved, his hair rose; when he moved, my hair did the same. He was much the larger of the two. I matched him up with my dining-room rug, and he went all right. I must likewise have harmonized with some color scheme of his, for he took a step towards me.

Remembering that my hunting knife was in the gunwale of the skiff and my rifle halfway across the bay, I closed the interview and went after them. It was a nice cool day and I hurried a bit. I felt light in the body and strong in the legs, which provoked in me a sudden disposition to disprove my previous theory that a two-hundred-pound man out of condition cannot outrun a bear. You see, this was the first bear I had encountered which really matched my furniture, and—in fact, there were sundry reasons why I increased my normal speed of limb.

To stroll means to advance carelessly. I strolled up to the skiff so carelessly that I nearly broke a leg getting into it, then headed for the launch. Perhaps a rear view had convinced the bear that my hair was too stiff, or that I was not sufficiently well furred for his use; at any rate, he did not pursue me, and in fifteen minutes I was back again and had taken up the trail. Two hours later I stumbled out of the woods, sweaty, smelling of blood, and supremely proud of a wet, heavy skin which dragged upon my aching shoulders, its points trailing on the ground behind me.

It had been a matter of a quick, careful search with the glasses, a brown blot creeping across an open meadow, a lung-bursting detour to leeward, and then a breathless descent of the mountain side, till a fringe of brown hair showed through the grass. There had been a quick guess at where the shoulder should be, a vision of snarling white teeth, and a great bulk lifting itself up towards me; another squint at a hairy chest between two huge forearms, and then three snap shots which were all too high and tore the sod as the fellow went lumbering down the hill. Next a sudden breaking down of the hind quarters, and twenty yards farther a loosening of all holds and a crash into the bed of a trickling gully.

As I gloated barbarically over the magnificent carcass, up from the woods across the bay came the

Although grizzlies aren't the blood-thirsty killers of fairy tales, precautions in grizzly range are necessary, for an encounter with a grizzly that feels threatened can be fatal. (Photograph © Michael Mauro)

sound of four quick, faint shots, "Bang! Bang! Bang! Bang!" as if Fred and Joe were answering my recent fusillade.

It took me an hour to finish the skinning, and as I reached the launch I heard wild shouting across the mud flats. On the fringe of the timber I saw the two boys.

"Somebody's hurt," exclaimed the engineer, but those yells carried a different note to me.

"They've got a bear!" I yelled, gleefully. "Fred has got one at last." And ten minutes later, while still a half mile distant, he began to tell me about it. I answered with my story, neither of us distinguishing more than the din of his own voice.

"I got—" came Fred's rejoicing, while the sun glinted on Joe's white teeth "—big grizzly, color—match—bungalow EXACTLY!"

Left: *A grizzly sleeps in the shallows of Alaska's McNeil River, where a concentrated population of grizzlies gathers annually to harvest the salmon run. (Photograph © Jeff Foott)*
Overleaf: *Grizzly bears are distinguishable from their less massive cousins, the black bear, by their distinctive muscular shoulder hump, visible in this grizzly even from afar. (Photograph © Dušan Smetana)*

THE ULTIMATE BULL

by Patrick F. McManus

Patrick F. McManus, famed humorist, grew up in the mountains of Idaho, a rural area touched by the Great Depression well past the 1930s. His self-described precarious childhood was in many ways idyllic for a kid: "I ran traplines, hunted with my own shotgun, fished every spare moment, roamed wild and free in the woods and mountains."

Aiming to combine this backwoods freedom with financial comfort, McManus decided to become a writer. "The way I figured it," he writes, "I could sit in a little cabin in the mountains of Idaho, write books and stories, mail them off to publishers, and they would mail me back big checks, and soon I'd become rich and famous." But after a decade spent struggling over serious-minded freelance articles, McManus had not yet made a name for himself, or much money off his writing.

His most significant sale came in 1968 when *Field & Stream* ran a humorous essay about wildlife he had dashed off in an hour. And thus his childhood outdoors—"happy in its sublime chaos and confusion"—became the fodder for hundreds of articles and over a dozen books. In the following story taken from his 1994 bestseller, *How I Got This Way*, McManus explains, in his classic whimsical style, how to bag—or make people think you bagged—a trophy elk or two.

L et me begin by saying that I don't hold with lying. It is a disgusting habit, with no other purpose than the deceit of one's fellow man and woman. After a lifetime spent in the company of elk hunters, I am pleased to report that they as a group abhor lying as much as I do. Oh sure, elk hunters are only human, and occasionally an innocent little fib will escape their lips while they're relaxing around the campfire of an evening.

A hunter might, for example, describe his packing of an elk quarter up a mildly steep hill in terms more appropriate to carrying a refrigerator up the north face of the Matterhorn. But that is an exaggeration to be forgiven. What cannot be forgiven is the outright lie, such as changing a five-point rack into an eight-point rack. That sort of unconscionable falsehood offends the honor of all elk hunters, who know that it is permissible to add only two points at most to a rack, and then only to a hunter's first elk. His future elk are not permitted to grow any points at all after they have been shot, unless, of course, the hunter has reached the age of sixty-five, and then anything goes.

First called wapiti by the Shawnee, this grand animal was later dubbed elk by European explorers for its resemblance to moose, or "elk," of their home continent. (Photograph © Dušan Smetana)

I know an elk hunter who upon turning sixty-five gave up the sport. Scarcely a month later, he had bagged at least a dozen more elk than I had been aware of, which was three, and I was both pleased and astonished to hear of his recent good fortune.

"Ed," I said to him, "I never realized you were such a successful elk hunter."

"Yes, I am," he replied simply.

"Here all the years we've known each other, you have only mentioned three elk. Now, suddenly, there are eighteen."

"Twenty-three."

"Ah, twenty-three now. I would have thought an even two dozen perhaps."

"I prefer the odd number. Besides, I'm too old to hunt down another elk."

"Really?" I said. "Why, I would judge that the last twenty elk were about the easiest ever taken in the entire history of hunting."

"Well, they were a heck of a lot easier than the first three, I can tell you that."

By age seventy, Ed was kicking himself for not having at least ten of his elk officially scored, because they would easily have made Boone & Crockett, with several possible world records.

Ed was a man of restraint, however, and once his lifetime score reached twenty-three elk, he held pat on that number and refused to exceed it, even though that would have been easy enough for a hunter of all the skills he'd acquired since giving up the hunt. Ed did not believe in excess.

One day as he was approaching ninety years, I asked him if he had bagged any of those elk with a bow.

"Not at the present time," he said.

So right there you can see how modest he was. He could just as easily have shot half those elk with a bow, but he wouldn't do it.

As I say, all true and honorable elk hunters under age sixty-five, and a few over, abhor the lie and will never use it to deceive their fellow elk hunters. What means are left, then, with which to deceive fellow elk hunters? Disinformation. Yes, disinformation. This is a wonderful rhetorical device developed by the folks in Washington, D. C., to avoid telling either lies or the truth. Here's an example of how disinformation can be put to good use by elk hunters.

This mature Montanan bull elk carries a massive 7×7 rack. (Photograph © Michael H. Francis)

Above: *The bull elk's mating call, or bugle, typically begins on a medium clear note, rises gradually to a high pitch, and ends in a shrill scream followed by a series of grunts. (Photograph © Alan and Sandy Carey)*
Facing page: *The furry velvet covering on this Rocky Mountain elk's rack is actually a soft, skin-like tissue that carries nourishment and calcium for the rapidly growing antlers. (Photograph © Bob Sisk/The Green Agency)*

Let us say that you got your elk last year by grace of your cow permit. You are now playing cards with some other elk hunters, and one of the guys asks you if you got your elk last year. You feel no pressing need to mention that your elk was a cow.

"Yup," you say. "Whose deal is it?"

"Harry's. Good rack?"

"Nothing I'd hang on the wall. I thought Harry just dealt. It must be George's deal. No? Well, let's see, I dealt two hands ago and . . . whoops! Sorry! Didn't mean to spill my hot coffee in your lap, Charlie."

That is how disinformation allows one to keep from telling a lie without telling the truth, augmented by a bit of diversion.

Now let's say that I am seated at a table at a Rocky Mountain Elk Foundation banquet, and I in all my years of dedicated elk hunting have never shot an elk. Naturally, I want to appear as adept at hunting elk as my banquet companions. Otherwise, what am I doing here at an elk-hunters' banquet? I certainly

don't want to be found out as an imposter. So what can I do? When all of the successful elk hunters of the previous year are asked to stand, I alone at our table remain seated. But I do not merely sit there. I also smile bemusedly. You can get a lot of mileage out of a bemused smile.

"No luck last year, huh?" one of the successful hunters asks me.

"Oh, I looked over some pretty good racks," I reply, "but nothing I wanted to pull the trigger on."

The reason I didn't want to pull the trigger on the racks is that they were hanging on a friend's wall, and he would have been mad as the dickens. Thus no lie is involved in this response, as you can see. My response is merely a bit of disinformation. Nevertheless, I have left the impression that I have reached the discriminating stage of elk hunting where only the ultimate bull will do. Impressed by this response, my dinner companions lean forward attentively, hoping to pick up a few tips from a master elk hunter. I must then launch into something like the following soliloquy in my best authoritative tones.

"The thing to remember about your really big bull is that he's almost never going to be where you want him to be. So you have to hunt him where you don't want him to be. And that's the steepest, nastiest hole in the mountains that you can find. You spend half a day climbing down into that hole, and there's your elk. Or maybe not. If he's not there—and you want to remember this—then he's someplace else. Most of the time, in fact, he's someplace else. Or maybe he's where you wanted him to be in the first place, but you are someplace else, namely where you didn't want the elk to be, and he isn't. That's pretty much the essence of elk hunting as I see it."

"Gosh, sir, how many elk have you got in your lifetime?" a young fellow asks.

"Not really all that many, son. Fewer than a dozen. [Like a dozen fewer.] But keep in mind, that I'm not going to take just any old bull elk that comes my way." [Like if a bull elk ever comes my way on roller skates, I'm not going to shoot him. Unless, of course, I think he stole the skates, which he probably did, because how else would a bull elk get roller skates? So I'd have to shoot him anyway.]

"What's the longest shot you've ever made?"

"I'd guess about six hundred yards." [Missed, of course.]

"Wow! What's your best rack, sir?"

"My best rack? Hmmmm, let me think. Yes, my best rack. Whose deal is it, anyway?"

"Deal? We're not playing cards."

"Good heavens, so we're not. I thought it was a terribly slow game. I must be at the wrong table. If you gentlemen will excuse me. . . ."

Now, here's a tough one. Suppose a friend asks you the location of your secret elk-hunting place. Your initial impulse is to lie: "What secret elk-hunting place? I don't have a secret elk-hunting place." But that would violate the elk-hunter's code. On the other hand, you know if you tell him your friend will invite all his cronies along with him, and they will chase all your elk into the next state. You could tell him to just buzz off and find his own secret elk-hunting place, but that would break the bonds of friendship, which would be all right, too, if the guy didn't hold the mortgage on your house on which you're behind three payments. So you must tell him.

"My secret elk-hunting place?" you say. "Henry, you are the only person in the world I'd reveal this to, even if you didn't hold the mortgage on my house, and you must promise never to tell another soul. Here's how you can get there. You drive up to the end of Jefferson Creek Road, and then climb to the top of Jefferson Peak. There's no trail, but just keep going up until you reach the peak. You can't miss it. Now, pay attention to this, Henry. Take a long rope. You'll need the rope to get down the sheer cliff on the other side of the peak. The rope

*A bull elk forages in a field in Yellowstone National Park.
(Photograph © Robert E. Barber)*

will also come in handy for hauling your elk back up the cliff. Once you're in the valley below, you'll see another mountain off to your right. Climb that one. Take a left at the top."

"Good gosh," Henry says, interrupting. "Isn't there a road anywhere near this secret elk-hunting place of yours?"

"Whose deal is it? I just dealt, didn't I? So it must be yours, Henry. Oops, sorry! Spilled my coffee right in your lap."

THE
FIRST

*"Running and bounding, his horns tossing, his white mane shining,
pranced a great bull caribou. I had seen deer in the woods at home,
but I had never known that an animal large as this could be so
wildly alive. . . . It was indeed my first sight of big game."*
—Edison Marshall, The Heart of the Hunter, 1956

MY FIRST
MOUNTAIN SHEEP

by Jack O'Connor

In all aspects of life, we reminisce about "the first," whether it may be our first rifle, first automobile, or first love. Our fondness for "firsts" is especially true in the world of big game hunting.

For veteran hunter Jack O'Connor, tracking caribou, moose, and grizzly bears were "an old story," as he writes in this tale. O'Connor had traveled far and wide through the breadth of the Alaskan wilderness over the years, and his trophies and experience were a testament to a lifetime of dedicated hunting. But his first trek up alpine slopes after a Rocky Mountain bighorn became an unforgettable experience, and he relished retelling the story throughout his life.

The following story is taken from the November 1945 issue of *Field & Stream*.

Prospecting is work. It's hard work, plenty hard, but it's the way a lot of fellows make a living. There's always the lure that you are going to hit it rich. That keeps a fellow going.

Ed Griffin and I had been prospecting throughout the summer on the drainage of the Little Delta River, a tributary of the Tanana, which drains a large part of the Alaska Range lying south of Fairbanks. Glacier-fed, this river heads in what was once perhaps the finest mountain sheep range in the whole world. At the time we were digging and sampling and hoping it was particularly well-stocked with mountain sheep. As we worked the animals were frequently in sight, and Ed and I were both looking forward to the freeze-up when we could conscientiously give up the search for riches and head into the peaks on an honest-to-goodness sheep hunt.

Pages 42-43: A bighorn ram in front of a mountain backdrop. (Photograph © Dušan Smetana)
Page 43, inset: W. S. Adams poses with his elk trophy near Fremont Lake, Wyoming. (Courtesy of the Wyoming Division of Cultural Resources)
Facing page: The bighorn is a wild sheep that lives in the mountains of western North America. Bighorns share domesticated sheep's hoofs, even toes, compartmentalized stomach, cud-chewing, and horns. (Photograph © Robert E. Barber)

Meriwether Lewis and William Clark, the American explorers who made their famed expedition to the Pacific in the early 1800s, were impressed by what they called the bighorn's "liquid amber eyes." (Photograph © Bill McRae)

That year the freeze-up came about the middle of September, and we called it quits, picking out the range that lies between the Little Delta River and Dry Creek for our hunt. Dry Creek is another tributary of the Tanana and runs at almost right angles to the Little Delta River, yet both streams head in the same mountains.

We had spent a good deal of time in this range, tracing float copper in an attempt to locate a ledge. During this time we had seen many large rams in the high hills. There was one particular ram which we had seen feeding high up on the upper reaches of the mountain, and we both had our hearts set on him. In fact, I had planned to make the trip up there alone if, for any reason, Ed had decided not to go after sheep or to hunt elsewhere. Our grub was getting pretty low, and this was another excuse, and a good

one, for us to stop prospecting and go after a little meat.

Neither of us had ever killed a mountain sheep, but we had both hunted and killed most of the other large game of the North. Caribou, moose and grizzly bears were an old story to us.

We decided to toss a coin to see who would get the first opportunity to crack down the big ram. I was lucky enough to win the toss. We sorted and re-sorted our packs, taking as little as possible with us. We knew that at night the thermometer would drop as low as zero and that it would be above freezing in the afternoons on the sunny side of the hills away from the breeze. When we were all set to go, our packs weighed about forty pounds each. This included a small tent, two bed rolls, rifles and grub.

We pitched camp at the very top of the timber

Above: *The bighorn is a cliff-dwelling animal that relies on easy access to avalanche chutes and talus slopes as its main defense against predators. (Photograph © D. Robert Franz)*
Overleaf: *Spanish explorer Francisco Vásquez de Coronado, the first European to explore the American Southwest, made the first recorded sighting of a Rocky Mountain bighorn in 1540. (Photograph © D. Robert Franz)*

near a patch of alders, where we could get a few dry twigs to start a fire. There was also dry grass in the creek beds to augment dry fuel, and we could keep a fire going with green wood. Fires, of course, at this altitude would only be used for cooking. When a fellow got cold, he went to bed.

That first morning in camp we were up long before daybreak and had a good breakfast of bacon and sourdough hotcakes and coffee. The left-overs were taken along for lunch, for we did not know when we would get back to camp.

The mountain was good and steep, and in the pitch-dark we had to take our time. That's where many fellows make a mistake in mountain hunting. There's nothing that will put you down and out quicker than going too fast. Frequently we would stop and rest and give our pumps a chance to get back to normal. That's the signal which nature gives a man when he is overdoing. When your pump begins to pound, it's the red light that means slow up.

As day began to break, we could see bands of ewes and young ahead of us, starting to feed. A lot of hunters say that a mountain sheep depends entirely upon its eyes and that it lacks the power of scent so keen in the deer family. I have always thought that was rubbish, and this trip proved it to be. These feeding bands of sheep paid not the slightest attention to us until the wind carried our scent their way. Just as soon as they got a whiff of man they rambled. In fact, they stampeded.

Here was a problem that we had to solve. With a band of racing, frantic ewes and lambs tearing along ahead of us we would never be able to get near any ram, let alone the old miser we were after. There was nothing to do but work around these bands of sheep so that they would not get our scent.

This led us over much loose shale rock, and we took plenty of time to negotiate the slopes. First, we wanted to be fresh when we reached the top and in condition to shoot accurately. Second, this shale wasn't the safest thing that a man ever walked on. Furthermore, there were occasional patches of snow that had to be crossed, and from freezing and thawing all summer they were as hard as ice—too hard to dent with a rifle butt. This meant that if you slipped on a dangerous slope you'd go places. Coming down,

we could go where we pleased, and we made a mental note of these steep, icy slopes in order to miss them on the return trip.

At about eleven o'clock I spotted a fine large ram lying on the edge of a cliff near the top of the highest peak. He was in a position to see almost any approach except directly over or behind him. Whether or nor he was the old ram we had been watching all summer was something we could not be sure about. We didn't waste much time wondering, however, as he was plenty big enough.

We had to work back down-hill to get under a cliff and go around to keep out of his sight before we could work up and above him. This was the tedious part of the hunt. You can't hurry. It's hard work, and you know that a vagrant puff of wind may carry your scent to the ram at any minute. There was a steady breeze blowing, but the winds can vary ever so little along a steep canyon, and often one puff will undo a whole day's hard stalking. I have seen an old ram raise and snort and stand at attention, looking and searching for the hunter when he got a whiff of man scent from far below. You can bet that very shortly every sheep on that part of the range got the signal that danger was close.

We carefully kept out of sight until we finally made the back of the hill, and worked up to where we could look down. The spot where our ram had been was vacant. He was gone. I did not know which way, whether he had just moved off to feed or whether he had seen or smelled us and left in a hurry. We scanned all parts of the valley. Sheep were feeding in various places; so we were satisfied that he had not been frightened, or he would have startled the others.

There was a draw running up the mountain which he might have taken and which would place him on the farther side of the hill, yet he would not have been able to see our approach. Slowly we worked our way along until about three hundred feet from the top. Here Ed motioned me to stop. He said he thought he saw another large ram away over on another hill and that he would stay there and watch it while I went to the top of the ridge to look the country over.

* * *

Alpine meadows and foothills are favored habitats for bighorn sheep. (Photograph © Neal and M. J. Mishler)

I climbed up near the top and then lay down and wriggled the last few yards. As I peeped over from behind a slab of rock to see what the other side had to offer I was looking right at the biggest mountain sheep I had ever seen. He was standing just a few yards over the ridge, intently watching something below him on the mountain-side. I looked where he was looking, and saw a large black bear feeding up the slope. This bear had certainly been my friend.

Cautiously I pulled my rifle up alongside, eased a cartridge into the chamber, looked the sights over carefully and raised it to my shoulder. Just as I checked the stock the ram swung his head around to see what was going on behind him. I know I didn't make a sound until the rifle cracked. The ram spun around, falling in a heap, but he jumped to his feet and came bounding toward me as though he hadn't been touched. I never saw a sheep run faster or steadier. I jumped up and fired point-blank into his body, driving him into a heap literally at my feet.

I yelled for Ed, but it wasn't necessary. He was almost at my side, rifle at the ready in case I had missed. He said he thought I had shot at a grizzly and needed his help, as it sounded as though I had not made a clean kill with my first shot.

I thought I had missed that first shot and could not understand how such a thing was possible, as I was certain I did not have buck fever. Nevertheless I had to take a lot of kidding from Ed as we dressed the meat. After taking off the cape and skinning the sheep for packing out, we examined the head and discovered what had happened to that first .30-06 slug.

I had aimed at the sheep's neck. Just as he turned far enough to look back I squeezed the trigger. The bullet had hit the base of the right horn, tearing out a chunk, and turned out. This had knocked the ram down, stunning him enough so that he did not see me when he started back over the hill where he was sure he would be in no danger. Had the bullet lodged and plowed on through, it would probably have spoiled the horn and ruined the head for a trophy. As it is, that head is one of the finest I have ever seen.

We ate our cold lunch on the top of the hillside, then got our packs ready to hit the trail to camp. The days were short, and darkness was coming as we started back down the trail. We knew we had a long, tough hike and, being smart mountain men, we took a short cut down a draw. This led us to a straight drop-off of some three hundred feet which we could not navigate. There was nothing to do but back-track, tired as we were.

We were too heavily laden to make good time, and we would not leave any of the pack behind; so we continued plugging ahead. Ed carried my rifle as well as his own and a good half of the ram. I had the other half on my back and the head in my arms. It was tough going. The last long mile was the toughest. Although we were tired and hungry, neither of us wanted anything to eat when we got to camp. I boiled some water, and we had a good drink of strong tea and then rolled in for the night.

On checking the head we found the spread was 25 inches, the base of the horns 14¾ inches, the curl 43⅛ inches on one horn and 43¼ on the other. This is not a record, but it's a trophy to be proud of.

We had worked much harder getting that ram and packing him off the mountain than at any time we were prospecting, but we enjoyed every minute of it. Fellows who like to hunt are that way.

Facing page: *The bighorn, like cows and other ruminants, often wears a meditative, contemplative look. (Photograph © Rich Kirchner/The Green Agency)*

Overleaf: *Horns are permanent structures consisting of a bony core covered with a sheath of keratinous material. This mature bighorn ram carries a much-coveted trophy on his head. (Photograph © Terry Berezan/Wilderness Images Ltd.)*

EXCERPT FROM
THE DEER PASTURE

by Rick Bass

Aside from simply being that which occurs before all others, "the first" can be defined as foremost in importance. For Rick Bass, an elusive whitetail buck is "the first," and the memory of hunting it leads in lucidity of detail, heartache, and nostalgic attachment.

Born in south Texas, Rick Bass grew up "absorbing stories and family lore from his grandfather during deer-hunting trips." After studying wildlife biology and geology at Utah State, Bass worked several years as an oil and gas geologist, later incorporating these experiences into his acclaimed *Oil Notes* (1989). Praised as a gifted young writer with an important voice, the prolific Bass has published eleven books and contributed countless articles to national magazines. From his isolated home in Montana's Yaak Valley, Bass now devotes himself full-time to writing, working on a continuous flow of newspaper editorials, letter-writing campaigns, essays, and books. An ardent environmentalist, Bass is also, as one critic says, "as likable a writer as you're ever going to meet on the printed page."

In the following essay, excerpted from his remarkable first book, *The Deer Pasture* (1985), Bass tells us of his initiation to the thrills and regrets of deer hunting in his beloved Texas Hill Country.

The hardest deer I ever hunted, I never got; he won, I lost. I can accept this; it bothers me not. I went into the broken rocks and cedars and mountains and canyons back on the East Side, into his country, and he beat me. I came back out, and he stayed. I didn't give him a name. I don't know why I didn't; most of the time, when a hunter becomes involved with a trophy buck like this one, he'll attach some name to the creature, something to add personality, something inevitably corny like Old Mossy Horns, or the Big Twelve Point, or even Old Grey-Deer. I didn't, though; this deer was too smart even to be named. Naming implies mortality. It is that marvelous streak of human nature that makes it seem as if once an object has been named and defined, it can be had, be it a mathematical equation, a strain of cancer, or whatever, and this was just not the case with this deer. He was unhaveable.

The most common North American deer is the whitetail. Its signature tail is almost a foot long and flourishes as a white "flag" when the startled deer leaps away. (Photograph © Doug Locke)

Also, I had never seen enough of him at one time to name. I saw his rubs on the cedar saplings, saw glimpses of him running back in the cedars, glints of horns, the deep prints he made in the sandbars down on the creek, his dew claws sinking in up to his hock—but I never saw him square on, not enough to define him. Naming also implies knowledge, and I just flat didn't know this deer. I suppose if I was to call him anything, it would have been "The Shadow," or something like that. Because even on my best days, when I got up my earliest and stalked my quietest and hid down in the rocks my stillest—even then, that was all I ever saw, really, the shadows of the places he had been, and then I would do something really stupid like blink or breathe or even make my heart start beating, and he would hear it or see it, and he wouldn't be there; the dark form I had almost seen through the cedars would suddenly no longer be there, and I'd know he was gone.

Sometimes, even in the middle of the brightest days, there are canyons and deep thick scrubs of cedar on the slopes of the near-vertical bluffs back on the East Side that are dark as twilight, spooky to be in by yourself. It's a long way from camp; it's the point furthest from the cabin. You run into our fence line but cross it, as we did pig hunting one night, and you get over onto Mr. Edgar Gold's old place, up the creek about two hundred yards, and suddenly you find yourself in the depths of a cataclysmic, exploded, twisted, contorted mass of boulders and tilted-vertical rock formations called Hell's Half-Acre. I think this is where that deer was living when I was hunting him, but he liked to cross the fence and nap in the shade of our cedars sometimes on the hottest days. I do not really think he was honestly one of our resident deer, which made him all the more coveted, all the more desirable.

I hunted him two seasons. The closest I ever got to him was on the third day of the first year, the day when, coming back down the hill, scuffling through the live oaks, feet crunching leaves, head down, daydreaming, thinking about lunch, just grinning, grinning like a teenager in love, just happy to be there, I discovered him. The wind was just right; it was lifting lightly up out of the creek bottom, far below, and he was on the mid-slope, napping.

He must have thought I was a whole herd of deer, I guess, moving slowly through the dead, dry oak

This whitetail lives in Montana, where archery season opens in early September and general and backcountry season ends in late November. As Havilah Babcock said, "My health is better in November." (Photograph © Alan and Sandy Carey)

leaves, or a cow, maybe, a big, slow, stupid, upwind and odorless cow. He knew I wasn't a hunter; hunters, he knew, tiptoed, or crept around semifurtively on the balls of their feet and clacked rocks and broke twigs every thirty steps or so, and then froze with fear after making such mistakes. Hunters, he knew, did not come sailing straight down the middle of the woods with not a thought in their heads.

As I have said, it was my first year to hunt the deer pasture.

I rather like to imagine the flat out-and-out alarm, consternation, and even rage, yes, rage—No fair! You're supposed to play by the rules! You're not supposed to make noise on purpose—that flared up in his eyes and in his mind when, with sickening stomach and lurching heart, he realized that I was neither herd of deer nor cow after all, but hunter, and that I was within rock-throwing distance of him before he discovered it.

I really was, I was almost upon him. I had left the oaks, gone across the meadow, and was down in the cedars, in his cedars, when I saw him.

I like to think it is the closest any human being has ever gotten to him.

I know it is the closest.

I could see the sleekness of his coat, and how golden butter tan it was, even in the shadows, where the few soft bars of sunlight that did shaft down through the overstory struck him, and I remember thinking, in a detached sort of way, how very odd it was that a deer that size should have such a light and golden coat; usually, in the Hill Country, the really big bucks have a darker coat, a light slaty color, even, sometimes. I remember thinking how oddly instinctive it was to be swinging my rifle up and putting the scope on him, smoothly, without thinking, as if there was a voice inside me going through all the steps involved, and that it was not me at all, but some deeper, ancestral urging, saying be calm, poise, raise, strike, harvest. I remember going through these motions calmly, confidently. I remember seeing the big deer crash straight through a row of wind-felled timber, branches popping and limbs snapping, giving it all or nothing, literally smashing his way

through a wall of logs and dead cedar, and then for a long, long time I could continue to hear his mad escape, and I remember thinking, well, if he had stayed around another four or five seconds, I would have shot him and killed the biggest buck Grandaddy had ever seen, the biggest buck ever killed in Gillespie County. I remember not being disappointed until about fifteen minutes later, walking on back to camp again, when, after getting over the initial marvel of just seeing such a magnificent creature, I began to mourn the fact that I had not gotten lucky, as they say, and beaten him. Won. Returned to camp the victor. The provider. Cries of excitement and adulation from the tribesmen. Hoopla and kudos and meat for a month, for all of us.

I somehow conveniently overlooked the fact that I had been lucky as stink just to have seen the big deer in the first place.

That was really the last time I ever saw him at all, running or otherwise. I haunted those cedars, hid everywhere imaginable. I stayed up in my hammock, twelve feet high, one night, to see if he moved through there at night when the moon was big. Anything, to try to pin him down for even a little clue, a little information into his private life. But he was unhuntable; he refused to participate.

I wasted a lot of time over on that mountain in those cedars and learned a lot about white-tails. Saw a lot of other deer. It's an interesting concept, going into an area and then just living there, practically, and paying intense and minute attention to every detail, learning it like, as they say, the back of your hand, and essentially forsaking all other areas—the Water-Gap, the Old Moss Tree, Buck Hill, the Pipeline. . . . I don't do it anymore; I wander everywhere, sort of taking the whole pasture in smorgasbordlike, but those first two years, with the memory of that big monster still exciting me every time I thought of him, I camped. I stuck tight to the very place I'd seen him. I became a student of that spot.

The closest I ever got to him again was the first day of my second season. He had gone back to the cedars; I was sitting there when the sun came up that first morning, sitting on a rock with both arms

Facing page: *This whitetail buck carries a 4×5 rack. (Photograph © Stephen Kirkpatrick)*
Overleaf: *Whitetailed deer are infamous for their ability to blend into their surroundings, freezing until even a seasoned hunter loses sight of the animal amidst its concealing environment. (Photograph © Michael Mauro)*

A whitetail with the velvet peeling from his rack on a late summer afternoon. (Photograph © Ann Littlejohn)

wrapped around me, breathing out smokeclouds even through my nose, and wondering what I could do about it. There was no way to make them turn invisible; you could see them a mile off—puff, puff . . . puff, puff. . . . I felt as if I was doing as much good as if I had been jumping up and down and shouting "Here I am! Here I am!"—when I saw that he was watching me. He was crouched down and motionless, like a wary thing, more like a feral dog or coyote than a deer. He was about thirty yards downslope, and he was behind some cedars along a little ridge of granite that ran at about a forty-five degree angle down the slope, through the cedars, and on across the creek and up another hill. He was watching me. I know now, I think anyway, that it was my imagination, but at the time, his eyes looked golden. Like a Weimaraner's, like a Labrador retriever's; they did not look like the eyes of a deer, and they did not blink. It was spooky. I think now it was just the morning sun coming up over my back. Back in the cedars, he was really just more of a silhouette than a form. You could

see him frozen there, studying me, evaluating me; you could see him weighing his options.

I watched his shadow watch me; you could see it was against his character to go charging wildly off into the brush when frightened, as did most other white-tails. As he did the first time he saw me. You could tell it was against his character to be frightened, too. He was not a panicky deer.

What he did was this: he sank down to his belly, down to the ground, so that he was behind that ridge of rock that ran through the new growth of cedars. Was it a fault scarp? The remnants of an old stone fence from settler days, or older? An eroded, exposed volcanic intrusion? Whatever it was, it was between two and three feet high, and sinking down behind it was like hiding behind a rock wall. A rock wall that ran all the way down the slope, to safety. All he had to do was make it down to the creek, crawling, of course, like a commando on hands and knees; but surely he wouldn't do that. Deer don't have minds like that, capable of understanding such abstract

A whitetail's antlers usually shed in January or February, although occasionally a buck will carry his rack as late as May. (Photograph © Bill McRae)

concepts as strategy and planning and the like. That deer wasn't able to look at the rock wall and know that if he stayed behind it, and stayed down, I couldn't see him. At best, he was probably sitting there, terrified, frozen, waiting for me to do something, something that would trigger his instinct and allow him to react. Deer, and other animals like them, are different from people; they merely react; they can't think, can't map out escape strategies. I knew he had sunk down behind those rocks and at that very moment was just cowering there, waiting for me to go away.

I was not going to go away. I was not really sure how I was going to do it at that close range, but I was going to stalk up to that rock fence in the woods, stand up, and there he would be, on the other side, point blank, the biggest deer ever seen on the deer pasture. What was the etiquette for such an occasion, for such a stalk? How did one kill a deer at such close range? With a Bowie knife? Would it be unfair not to let him spring up and run twenty yards or so? Was it hard to get the scope on a running deer that is crashing through the brush only twenty yards away? Would it even be sportsmanlike to risk such a shot at a difficult, moving target? What if I hit him in the leg, the shoulder, or, God forbid, the stomach? What if I missed? But if I didn't let him run—if I surprised him—would I actually shoot him from three or four yards away? Was that fair, either?

Needless to say, that was the last I ever saw of that deer. Still not sure of my plans, I sank to my own knees on the other side of the rock fence and began creeping towards it, very quietly, very slowly. I paused often; my heart was hammering. I knew he was just on the other side of the fence, right where I had seen him go down. I was the picture of stealth. I was silent, invisible. It was the most perfect stalk ever made. Even as I reached the fence and then quickly rose up over it, steeling myself for his startled reaction—even then I am not sure what I had in mind

doing. Tackling him, I suppose, or wrestling him 'til he said uncle, I don't know.

Only he wasn't there. I couldn't believe it. It was more than embarrassing; it was devastating. It was impossible to look at the spot without feeling the burning realization that the entire time I had been crawling slowly and on my belly across the ground, that during the entire stalk, he had been long gone, and that I had been sneaking up on an empty patch of Gillespie County. That I had pounced on an empty piece of Hill Country.

I walked up the rock ridge; I walked down it. I looked everywhere, as if I might have just missed him, overlooked him, and he was not gone at all but still on the mountain, right under my gaze, as a set of keys or a pair of scissors are in your desk at work when you really need them, and you rummage back and forth over them several times in the clutter without really seeing them, you are looking for them so hard. That is how I surveyed the woods all around me then. As if the biggest deer in the county had not given me the slip but was indeed still there, hiding camouflaged against a patch of deer-colored boulder or something, still waiting for me to leave.

I left, all right. I was sick.

Also, I never saw him again.

And I never hunted that area again, either.

I've got no truck with that deer anymore; he beat me fair and square and soundly; I know my limitations. So now I hunt Buck Hill and the Burned-Off Hill, and I range and roam and see lots of different sights, lots of different deer, and I beat some and get beaten by others.

But I never forget the big deer over on the East Side that I didn't even see enough times to give a name to. The first deer I ever tried to hunt specifically, in Gillespie County, in the Texas Hill Country. The first deer that ever beat me, in Gillespie County, in the Texas Hill Country.

Facing page: *Whitetailed deer prefer habitat with extensive forested cover, though they are also inhabit grasslands, especially where varied elevations of wetlands provide cover. (Photograph © Doug Locke)*
Overleaf: *This whitetail buck shows off his petite ears, which are much smaller than those of his long-eared cousin the mule deer. (Photograph © Stephen Kirkpatrick)*

Chapter 3

BIG GAME
COUNTRY

"The basin is like a great bowl with one side broken out in a jagged gap towards the east, where the creek draining the place takes a dizzy plunge fifteen hundred feet into the canyon below, and then goes twisting down between the mountains towards the Waterton River. For want of a better name we will call it Paradise Basin, which is whispering-close to adequate."
—Andy Russell, Horns in the High Country, 1960

ANTELOPE CAMP

by Tom Carpenter

Tom Carpenter has two passions: the outdoors and writing. Wisconsin born and raised, he "hunted the ridges, valleys, and riverbottoms of the state's southwestern corner" from the age of seven. Carpenter now makes his home in Minnesota, yet he is drawn to the Wyoming prairie every fall, to the "wide open spaces of the Great American West," to hunt pronghorn.

As the director of the North American Outdoor Group book development department, he edits a wide variety of hunting, fishing, and other books. In his writing, Carpenter attempts to "evoke the great outdoors and the feelings, moods and emotions experienced *out there,*" in big game country.

The author of *Images of the Hunt: Big Game* (1998) and *Mule Deer: Hunting Today's Trophies* (1998), Carpenter is currently working on a book about hunting pronghorn and regularly contributes his articles about hunting pronghorn, whitetailed deer, and mule deer to outdoors magazines. The following story, set in the windswept western plains, originally appeared in the September 1997 issue of *Wyoming Wildlife.*

For some hunters, an antelope is a novelty. Head to Wyoming once, maybe twice in a hunting lifetime and tack on an antelope license to whatever bigger, more glamorous game you have in mind. There's a head on the wall and a story to tell.

For others, an antelope is a commodity. Pronghorn season is a necessary inconvenience. It gets in the way of the other hunts that fill an autumn, but it is a good way to put meat by. Pick out a decent buck, get him in the cooler, and get on with the business of other game.

But to a precious few, antelope season is *the* hunt of the fall, and the antelope camp tradition is the highlight of the outdoor year.

You don't hear much about antelope camp in the popular sporting press. A tent in the sage and a crawl through rocks and prickly pear after pronghorns doesn't seem to compete with wall tents and elk in the lodgepole, backpacking for mule deer at timberline, a deer shack in the woods or a warm motel bed followed by fields full of pheasants. But me, I'll take the prairie, windy solitude and pronghorns.

Pages 70-71: *An Alaskan caribou in velvet. (Photograph © Stephen Kirkpatrick)*
Page 71, inset: *A herd of pronghorn race across the Wyoming prairie. (Courtesy of the Wyoming Division of Cultural Resources)*
Facing page: *The pronghorn "antelope," which is unrelated to the African antelope, inhabits the western North American plains. (Photograph © Jeff Foott)*

That's where antelope camp starts—way *out there* on some lonely stretch of dusty prairie road where my brother and I meet in the middle ground called Wyoming. From here, our pickups rattle and bounce through the late afternoon sun as we cruise the grasslands in search of "the spot."

The advantages to making camp out on the prairie range from the functional (you're right there with the antelope and can be hunting as soon as you put on your pants in the morning) to the esthetic (a moonlit, midnight walk down a prairie two-track, the scent of sage riding the cool night air, is probably as close as I'll ever get to paradise). But self-preservation prevails when choosing the spot where we raise our tent, and the name of the adversary here is wind.

It's impossible to avoid wind altogether, but we find ways to hide a bit. Usually this means settling on the lee side of some prairie geography—often in a cut to the south or east of some rim. Here we enjoy some shelter from the west and northwest breezes while staying at some elevation to avoid the pooling of the coldest air if the night breezes die.

Here we pitch our tent and then back up one truck nearby, tailgate down, as a cooking area. A camp table, grill and coolers round out the scene.

Then, as the sun dips below the rim, we clear out an area and dig a fire pit. Sitting in lawn chairs, our boots to the fire and our backs to the endless night, we warm our feet until the prospect of down sleeping bags on good air mattresses gives us enough courage to kill the fire and brave the frosty trip to the tent.

Now that we have been blessed with an addition to antelope camp—my teenage nephew Chuck, namesake of his father—the tent is a bit more cozy. But I still take my spot next to the far end, zip down a corner flap to the stars and sage, and wait for the bag to warm and sleep to come.

No alarm clocks on the prairie. As the dawn sky brightens and works its way into the tent, sleep leaves the three of us one by one. When all the snoring has stopped or breathing patterns have shifted, someone works up the courage to say, "Let's go."

There's not much time between waking and hunting. The downright chilly temperatures contribute to that in two ways. First—dressing is a shivering scramble. Second—an antelope camp breakfast is on-the-go. We learned long ago that a jug of orange juice, some fruit and a box of pastries en route to and between the most preferred antelope pastures is better than standing around trying to cook and eat in the frigid dawn, getting cold and wasting valuable hunting time.

Don't let anyone tell you different—early hunting is prime hunting. The pronghorns are out. They aren't as skittish when the sun is still below or just peeking over the horizon. You can use that low light to your stalking advantage as another source of "cover," this one over your back, on the wide-open prairie. And without mirage from the day's heat, the black horns of dark-faced bucks are easier to judge.

And so begins the hunt.

We'll stalk a strategic spot as often as we will an actual pronghorn buck. Each method offers a special excitement, the bottom line being the stalk itself: Planning it carefully and then sneaking close through the available topographical and vegetative cover without spooking an animal that can spot the slightest bit of movement at a mile is the essence of antelope hunting.

When stalking a strategic spot, we follow a sequence something like this.

It's our third morning of hunting. We've pulled off a few good stalks but backed off each hillside and dusted ourselves off, deciding to continue the fun and look for a bigger buck. A scouting walk on the prairie three evenings ago and a spot-check two days ago revealed a good-sized herd of does without a buck, residing in a secluded draw a mile from any two-track.

As the sun rises over our right shoulders, we walk upright, then crouched at the waist and finally on our hands and knees. As we near the final rise from where we can see into the basin, we crawl on our bellies and then peek over.

There they are. One, two, three . . . twelve . . . fifteen does. "There's a buck," big Chuck whispers, and my eyes pass beyond the does to a buck standing on a knoll, surveying his newly claimed harem. There is no need to study him further—his thick horns rise nicely and hook into a handsome heart shape. This is a nice, mature buck.

A pronghorn buck usually grows horns between twelve and eighteen inches long. (Photograph © Michael H. Francis)

I settle into the shooting sticks. My shot whizzes over his back. He ignores it in the howling wind, jogs down off the knoll and promptly mounts a doe. The does continue milling, and after five minutes they finally allow another clear look at the buck. My second shot is on its way and finds its mark.

As we walk up to the buck, I think: It's hard for antelope to not be beautiful, even in death. Stretched out in the sage, with one hoof out to take his last step, the pronghorn looks every bit as graceful as I'm sure he was speeding across the prairie.

When stalking an actual antelope, the sequence goes something like this.

We're rounding a bend in the old two-track we're driving, heading for a new section of prairie to explore. Our eyes glance up a draw as it begins to open into view, and we all see white pronghorn bellies and rumps at once. Truck in reverse, we back behind the hillside, plan our route for a minute, then start the long walk across the sage.

After a mile's hike, a mule deer doe and her twin fawns watching us the whole way, we kneel behind the especially-dense knot of sage we had chosen as our destination. There are well over a dozen antelope does 250 yards ahead, some bedded and some feeding, but no buck in sight. Three more does, only 50 yards ahead, block any further approach.

We get young Chuck set with shooting sticks, and I let out a big wheeze on my antelope call. A buck jumps from his bed in a gully, looking for his challenger. As we estimate the range, Chuck nestles in to

the 6mm. At the shot, the buck takes off untouched, steering his harem across the rolling prairie.

We follow them for the rest of the morning, playing a lopsided game of hide-and-seek that the antelope have no trouble winning before our legs give out. We're tired but think: What a great stalk, a morning on foot in the immensity of the prairie. It's the way the game should be played.

The successful stalks are, of course, the most exciting to tell about. But the truth is, most stalks don't even develop to the point where one of us can take a shot or whisper, "Let's go look for another one." Usually the antelope make the decision for us—winding us in a wild gust of prairie wind, catching the movement as a human head peeks over the crest of a ridge, or spotting some aspect of our motley trio of hunters, rifles and daypacks traveling through the sage on feet, knees or bellies.

By early afternoon we're hungry and ready for a rest, so we head back to camp for the day's big meal. Cooking, eating and clean-up is easier in the light and warmth of day, versus doing it tired at night. Tacos, steaks over sage-sprinkled charcoal, hamburgers, fajitas, fresh vegetables, salad . . . we eat well. There's no reason not to, when you can haul it to camp in your vehicle instead of on your back. A siesta is not unheard of, from hunters and antelope alike, during this midday lull. In any event, eyes and legs just need a rest.

As the sun descends and the shadows lengthen, we head out again. The antelope are usually more active now, and some evenings it seems as if they emerge out of nowhere—bands and bucks you didn't know existed—to places that were so empty earlier in the day.

Being *out there* now—with night coming on and the wind lying low and the big quiet so loud in your

Left: *Territorial pronghorn bucks aggressively defend their harems, and brief fights occasionally result in serious injury. These bucks were photographed sparring in Alexander Basin, Montana. (Photograph © Erwin and Peggy Bauer)*
Overleaf: *When a pronghorn feels threatened, the white hairs of its rump stand erect, producing a white flash that is visible for many miles on the sunny plains. (Photograph © Jeffrey Rich)*

A pronghorn buck. (Photograph © Michael H. Francis)

ears until they get used to the idea—is the loneliest time of day on the prairie. Of all the wonders of antelope camp, the evenings are the memories I take with me back to my non-prairie life in towns and the northwoods.

These are the times we'll see the gray mulies—where were they all day?—so graceful in the sage, coyotes—like them or not—trotting across the flats, a meadowlark flushing from the grass, a sage hen running almost soundlessly ahead as you sneak up a draw.

My nephew shot his first antelope on such a Wyoming evening.

We came upon the buck—a nice one—closely trailing a single doe in the last rays of sunlight peeking between a cloud bank and the Atlantic Rim. Chuck set up carefully and leaned into the shooting sticks. The buck began trotting off at Chuck's first shot, but the young hunter stayed calm as he worked the bolt. I called to the buck, he stopped to look back,

then it was over as the rifle made its odd, hollow "whump" in the huge silence.

The pronghorn looked pumpkin-orange and snow-white as we slowly walked up to him in the final glints of the half-sun raking across the sage, and another big game hunter was born.

It's dark by the time we pull into camp, the truck's headlights sweeping across a grassy hillside and finally stopping to rest on the lonely tent. We light the lantern; build a fire to ward off the cold; clean up the day's dust from faces, hands and equipment; and finally relax by the fire with sandwiches and snacks.

Once our re-living of the day's hunt is over and the strategy for the next day is set and we've covered various topics of importance and unimportance—almost all related to hunting—we'll once again brave the trip to the tent one by one, the last hunter dousing the fire for good.

If it's a day I've chosen to shoot and if I have been

A pronghorn horn consists of a bony core and a black outer sheath. The sheath sheds each year, making the pronghorn the only animal in the world to annually shed its horns. (Photograph © Michael H. Francis)

lucky, I'll smell a little like antelope—somewhat musky, a little sweet and a little salty and quite a bit like sage—as I curl up in the sleeping bag again. One of my brethren might wisecrack in the dark, "Somebody turn an antelope loose in here?" And I'll think, I'm too tired for a comeback.

But not every antelope camp night is idyllic. I'm referring in particular to the year antelope camp moved to the Motel 6 in town.

Now, September weather in Wyoming can be as lovely as God ever created—frosty clear dawns, warm sunny days, cool but bearable nights. Or it can be downright unpredictable and miserable. One particular year chose to offer us a little bit of both.

The second sunny afternoon of hunting finds us high on a secluded ridge, carefully playing cat-and-mouse in its folds with a nice buck and his band of does. When a couple snowsqualls hit, we don't worry; the sun breaks out after each one. Then a band of snow hits that doesn't stop in the usual 15 minutes. By the time we find our way back to the truck, we are soaked, and a couple inches of the white stuff are on the ground.

We slip and slide the truck back to camp—now covered under three inches of slushy snow—and say to hell with it. We grab a cooler of food and a change of clothes, drive 30 miles to town and spend the evening in our long underwear in warm motel beds, laughing at bad movies on cable TV.

I feel guilty for a little while (just a little while) thinking, "We should be toughing it out, *out there* on the prairie." But every time the wind roars louder, the guilt ebbs a bit more. Like that other antelope camp, this too is much different from everyday life!

When we bundle ourselves up to face 30-mile-per-hour wind gusts and 14° F cold the next morning, we further congratulate ourselves on our survival skills. We are alive, we feel good, we feel like hunting, and by mid-afternoon the temperature is in the 40s and the only snow left is in the shade on the north slopes and the prairie is habitable (for mere men) again.

Just as a little bit of snow can't end antelope camp, the shooting of an antelope does not signal its end either.

One memento I treasure as much as the memories, prime pronghorn venison on the grill at home, horns on the wall or pictures in a photo album, is the product of our annual video hunt. These stalks are every bit as exciting as those with rifle in hand, and in many ways are even more challenging because our camera's zoom lens doesn't have near the range of a .30-06.

We'll spend a day doing this—exploring the prairie, maybe poking around an old coal mine or abandoned homestead, stalking antelope bands when the whim hits us and the opportunity presents itself. It's just plain, no-worries fun, and we learn so much about pronghorn behavior: bucks sparring then chasing across the prairie in clouds of dust; does and fawns vocalizing to one another; a buck relentlessly bird-dogging a "hot" doe back and forth across a basin; a late fawn trying to sneak a quick suckle from her dam's udder; bucks issuing their snort-chuckle challenges to each other.

And after the antelope have been harvested but before the trip is over we'll just once go "herdin' antelope," as my nephew coined the activity several years ago. Sooner or later, in pronghorn country, a small herd will meet you and run parallel to your vehicle as you jostle along some secondary road or ranch road. We accept the challenge and punch our own accelerator, laughing and marveling at the fleet pronghorns stringing it out next to us.

Pronghorns just don't like to lose a race. So when the speedometer hits 35 miles-per-hour or so (as fast as we dare to go on a rutted back road or trail), they pour it on and zip across the road in front of us, then run straight away from the vehicle, their white rumps waving good-bye.

By the time we look back a second or third time, the antelope are standing way *out there* in the sage, staring at our dust plume, probably wishing we'd come back and race once more so they could beat us again.

That's always my wish—to come back again—as we pull antelope camp and then drive out along the lonely, dusty roads, once again in separate vehicles. Our good-byes are always short because we are men and because we didn't come to say good-bye to each other. We came to be together in antelope camp, and

Above: *This pronghorn lives in Montana's National Bison Range, established by Theodore Roosevelt in 1908 to provide sanctuary for the remnants of the great herds of buffalo that once covered the West. (Photograph © Jeffrey Rich)*
Overleaf: *Pronghorns have roamed the plains and deserts of the West for at least the last million years. (Photograph © Dušan Smetana)*

those are the memories we take home.

The good-byes are short for another reason too: because we always hope this is not the last antelope camp. I love a good rifle, wide open spaces, the prairie and the antelope that live there, and hunting with people I love. Carrying that rifle all day, walking the wide open prairie and seeing what's over every next hill, watching antelope live their lives for a few wonderful days . . . this is the calendar spot that truly marks the end of each year, and thus the beginning of another, for me.

And, later on, when times are tough—when winter has me down and cabin fever sets in, when pressures of work and mortgages and kid-raising and everything else that fills life today become almost too big to bear and sleep is hard in coming—my thoughts will drift to antelope camp. I'll see the open prairie, hear the wind in the sage, sling a rifle across my back and start walking.

CARIBOU DREAM

by John Barsness

A renowned figure in contemporary outdoors writing, Barsness has written from his native Montana for over twenty-five years. "Aside from writing, I've spent my life punching cows, cutting wheat, catching fish, and hunting edible animals," says Barsness, whose ties to the land are apparent in his literature.

His stunning *Life of the Hunt*, a collection of big game hunting adventures around the world, was praised by the editors of *Sports Afield* as "the single best hunting book" of 1995. His other books include *Western Skies* (1994), *Montana Time: The Seasons of a Trout Fisherman* (1992), and *Hunting the Great Plains* (1979).

Largely a freelance writer but also a staff writer for *Field & Stream* and *Gray's Sporting Journal*, Barsness focuses on "people who live on the land: Native Americans, farmers, ranchers, hunters, fishermen, and gatherers." As he explains, "My main interest is in the way the land shapes us, and how we shape the land." In this tradition, the following original story explores Arctic big game country, where the soil pre-dates life and caribou still travel in great migratory herds.

There's something fascinating to humans about herds of animals so large they cover the landscape like a moving web. As a little kid I could see, through some inward eye, thousands of buffalo galloping across the plains of my native Montana, and on television saw the vast wildebeest herds of the Serengeti and the caribou migrations of the north. As I grew older some illusions fell away. I knew I'd never see huge buffalo herds, despite the fact that Yellowstone Park's bison population was growing beyond its bounds. The possibility of seeing the Serengeti grew more real, but by then I knew it was another Yellowstone, the herds invaded by roving vehicles full of tourists, many of them shopping addicts disguised as wildlife photographers.

But caribou still roamed the north country, above and beyond civilization. I could see them up there, in the wide-angle lens of my mind, moving over the treeless hills like the antlered currents of a river. *Someday*, I thought, *someday I'll see them*. Of course this would be with the hunter's complex version of sight: pursuit and capture, holding those impossible antlers and actually making a caribou part of me, by eating flesh formed from tundra lichen. Caribou rested there for decades, in the jumble of my imagination, a northern dream.

The term "caribou" encompasses any of several large reindeer native to northern North America. Exotic quarry to most hunters in the Lower 48, caribou are Alaska's most-hunted big game. (Photograph © Dušan Smetana)

Caribou bulls and cows both carry large, branched antlers. (Photograph © Gary A. McVicker)

And then one September, three months before my fortieth birthday, I buckled myself into one of the rear seats of a Twin Otter float plane, in front of several lashed-down drums of diesel fuel and beside a pile of duffel bags and rifle cases, on the shoreline of Great Slave Lake in the Northwest Territories. The Otter tuned up, hearable even through foam ear plugs, feelable through the canvas seat, and smellable through the exhaust that seeped slightly through the windows. For a few minutes, as we planed across the lake and rose above the shacks and piles of fuel drums along the lake shore, I still felt enclosed by civilization.

And then we were free. The Otter reached a cruising altitude five hundred feet above the earth, the noise and vibration and exhaust tapered off, the shacks and oil drums disappeared, and the one lonely dirt road through the spruce and birch ended and we floated above a world totally empty of shopping malls and pop-top cans and computer chips. The land was not so much land as irregular islands and peninsulas, covered with dark-green spruce and yellow-leaved birch, curving and jutting into the nickel-bright lakes of the Territories. I sat with my forehead against glass and looked down, knowing this uncivilized world didn't end for literally thousands of miles, up and across the Arctic ice cap and down the other side of the world into the spruce and birch of Siberia.

We flew low enough to see individual trees and soon I noticed something hunters notice—trails. There were trails through the shallow swamps on the edges of the long peninsulas, and trails on the gravel ridges. The trails separated and braided, a steady thread joining the land from north to south. Down in civilization they might be cattle or sheep trails, but up here they could only be made by caribou.

And then the trees ended. The lakes were still nickel-blue but the land turned red-orange, covered with the dwarf forest known as tundra, made of shin-high huckleberry and willow. The Otter droned on and I watched the trails through the red tundra, and saw them.

There were perhaps six caribou, trotting through a trail-braided bog, the lowland between two ridges, and toward the rear was a bull. In our time we grow used to seeing things through the technology of film and television, and of course I'd seen caribou there before. But no film can ever prepare you totally for reality, for a caribou bull's high curve of antler, like a primitive dancer's headdress, so huge it seems added, not part of the animal. Or the tundra spring in the trot of a herd, as if the dwarf forest pushes them upward slightly with each step. Or the smallness of even a big bull in that infinite space of red tundra, because infinite is what it seems. A hundred-mile circle of horizon can be seen from even a low-flying Twin Otter—which in twenty minutes will be another hundred-mile circle, as empty of civilization as the last. As the caribou dropped behind us I suddenly knew I was in the circle of the dream.

When we finally landed at the camp, a cluster of white tents next to a long lake, it didn't seem strange that most of the people that greeted us were Inuits with names like Anthony Oogak and Samuel Takkiruq. By then I knew that I was Up There, in another country, and as we stowed our gear and were assigned guides and grew used to walking around on the ancient gravel of the Precambrian Shield—gravel so old it didn't contain animal fossils—I felt in no hurry. Partly this was because we'd already been informed we couldn't hunt the day we flew, in accordance with the laws of the Territories. But partly it was because I could feel the caribou coming, not in some mystical way, but through the cleaned skulls with their extravagant antlers lying around the camp, and the huge tracks on the hill above.

We went there in the evening, Anthony Oogak and I, and looked for caribou, and at dusk saw a herd of forty, mostly bulls, with one toward the rear standing out like a yacht in a fleet of shrimp boats. They were almost a mile away, but through the 30X spotting scope the tops of his antlers swept back like sails. Other groups of caribou came before and after the big bunch of bulls, and I felt no rush to hunt. It was enough to sit there, on the ancient gravel, and watch them come.

I killed a caribou the first day we hunted, though thankfully not out of the big group that came by as we beached the boat a half-hour from camp. That herd was made of cows and calves, and trotted by so closely we could hear the clicking of their hooves in

the gray light, so many that the sound was almost like the hiss of a snake winding through the tundra. Then we walked up through the rounded boulders and deep caribou paths to the hill beyond and watched the caribou come.

They didn't blanket the land, but came in patchy waves, like an old handmade quilt that's been handed down so many generations that your elbows and knees poke through. In this case the elbows and knees were the ridges of the tundra, and the remnants of the quilt moved around them in tatters of six and a dozen and three dozen. We watched and watched, and I asked Anthony about his life on an island above the mainland Territories, where the sea lay frozen for eleven months a year, where he hunted seals and wolves and polar bears and fished through several feet of Arctic ice for trout and char.

And then a group of bulls showed along a small lake a half-mile to the north. It was noon and the day warm and the seven bulls stopped and fed for a while, then lay down and we stalked them. The downwind path lay around the lake shore, where we found fresh grizzly tracks, large and small, sow and cubs. We then looked behind us as much as in front. The rule of thumb about grizzlies is the smaller they are, the meaner they get, a rule attributable to how tough it is to make a living. Along the Alaska and British Columbia coast they grow large and fat and mellow on salmon. In the mountains of Montana they grow half as large on marmots, berries and occasional elk calves—and twice as mean. In the Territories they grow very small on even less, and frighten even Inuits who hunt polar bears with .243s.

So our caribou stalk was doubly exciting, though we were just as glad not to find a bear stalking us. When we eased over the last rise on our hands and knees, the antlers of the herd rose only one hundred yards away. We could see all but the antlers I'd picked out through the spotting scope, so kept stalking until the herd rose and trotted in a half-circle around us, as precise as the half-circle of the tundra horizon. Then they stopped and looked at us, wondering what kind of caribou we were. At the sound of the .280 they trotted again, but after thirty feet one

faltered, then stopped, head swinging in another half-circle, and went down.

This began one of the more fascinating hours of my hunting career. We took a bunch of photos, which Anthony was more than happy to do. Many guides rush through the photo session, wanting to get on with the skinning and packing, but Anthony explained that he liked caribou to bloat slightly: the tight skin made precise caping easier. They bloat as fast as helium balloons, due to the gas produced by their diet, and by the time we started skinning this one was as tight as jeans on a grizzly bear.

Anthony used a knife as if it were part of his hand, like an over-large, sharpened fingernail. He caped the caribou in perhaps ten minutes, cutting around the eyes and lips, then skinned the back half, laying the hide hair-side-down on the tundra. Only then did he gut the bull, afterwards slicing off the shoulders and hind legs as easily as a chef dissects a chicken. He asked if I knew how to bone. When I nodded he started me on the hind legs, while he did the front. I asked how many caribou he butchered a year and he said oh, maybe a hundred. He said they were all good to eat, but bull hides made the best sleeping robes, and cow hides the best clothing. He was thirty-two, and until his tenth year he'd lived in igloos in winter and caribou skin tents in summer, traveling by dog team with his family across the tundra and Arctic Ocean. Caribou were their life, as much as bison had been the life of the Plains Indians.

In the end we slid the boned meat inside the rib cage, wrapping it in the back-skin. Anthony tied up the package exactly like a Rocky Mountain elk guide would manty up a hay bale, then attached a strap to the package and slung the strap over his forehead. I packed the cape and head, and we set off toward the lake, two miles away, a caribou on our backs.

And that is how the days went. Everyone in camp had two tags, and even after I killed my second bull, one with antler tops very much like whirling sails, I simply had to go along and sit on the pre-fossil gravel and watch the caribou come. I couldn't keep myself from helping Anthony skin and butcher caribou bulls, marveling at the variety of his skill and at the infinite variety of caribou antlers, as alike and un-alike as snowflakes.

I discovered that the tundra, even without cari-bou, was not the empty northern desert it appeared. Caribou antlers and bones were scattered every-where, and I began to see the smaller Arctic animals: vole, ptarmigan, hares. The camp filled with antlers and cheesecloth bags of meat, hanging along poles in back of the tents like another concentration of caribou. I ate caribou backstrap and heard the howl of a wolf, and lay on ridges eating dwarf huckle-berries while the waves of caribou built, like the waves building in front of a winter wind, and finally could make a guess about how it must have been when the first men chased wildebeests across the Serengeti and the First Americans chased bison across the shortgrass prairies. I fell asleep at night and rarely dreamed, partly because I was tired but partly because in the morning I knew I'd be living a dream, one of the oldest we can claim, so old it has almost been forgotten, even by hunters, the caribou dream.

This barren ground caribou bull lives in the Alaska Range of Denali National Park. (Photograph © William H. Mullins)

Chapter 4

TOILS OF
THE HUNT

*"Out before light, back after dark, a long day in the black timber beyond
the reach of humanity, with only the tiny voice in your head to break
the white-hot focus on each second, each sound, sight, and scent."*
—Chris Madson, "A Day Out," 1991

A BOWHUNTING (OB)SESSION

by Bill Heavey

To hunt for big game requires a particular kind of person—one willing to sweat, toil, and obsess. Bill Heavey exhibits this mindset in the following story, as he succumbs to the newfound lure of bowhunting whitetails.

Born in Birmingham, Alabama, and raised in Bethesda, Maryland, Heavey is a contributing editor at *Field & Stream,* where "A Bowhunting (Ob)session" first appeared in June 1998. A freelance writer based out of Arlington, Virginia, Heavey contributes his work, including essays, profiles, travel pieces, and outdoors articles, to the *Washington Post, Men's Journal, Reader's Digest,* the *Los Angeles Times, Washingtonian,* and *Outside,* among other magazines.

Heavey, who "first fished the Potomac River at the age of six," has since exhibited his bent toward the outdoors—and the toils of the hunt—in his writing. "I write," he says, "about the things I love."

I found the only other guy at the party who wasn't wearing a tie. Pretty soon we were talking bass and trout, ducks and doves. It wasn't long before he was telling me about bowhunting for whitetails. "Any dolt with a scope and a rail to rest his rifle on can shoot a deer at 300 yards," he insisted, swirling the bourbon in his glass. "Shooting one that's so close you can see his whiskers . . . now that's a different deal."

A little orange flare arced up in a dark cave in my brain. *You could do this,* it signaled.

"You don't need a bow named after nuclear weapons, military aircraft, or Clint Eastwood characters," my newfound friend continued, slowly reeling me in. "If it has the word *turbo* in it, pass. Any compound out there has the power to turn a monster whitetail into chipped venison."

Thus began my descent into bowhunting obsession.

The next week, after asking around, I settled on a PSE Nova, an entry-level one-cam. I went out and promptly began burying arrows in the back lawn. It was humbling to watch a 30-inch shaft disappear so fast you couldn't be sure you'd really owned that particular arrow

Pages 96–97: *A whitetail buck bedded in a forest. (Photograph © Doug Locke)*
Page 97, inset: *Sergeant Otto Hofer, Fourteenth Cavalry, and deer party near Eagle Pass, Oklahoma. (Courtesy Western History Collection, University of Oklahoma Libraries)*
Facing page: *This 4×5 whitetail buck shows off the large, white-fringed tail that gave the species its name. (Photograph © Dušan Smetana)*

in the first place. Then I discovered that I'd stored my bow upside down before tightening the sight pins. I fiddled with them, worked my way back to 20 yards, and began smacking the target consistently.

"Hooked" would be an understatement. I was filleted, battered, and deep-fried. It was like having a rifle with a silencer on it. My bag target actually shuddered under the impact of every shot. I loved the feeling of stored energy in the bow's limbs as the let-off kicked in, the Zen of relaxed strength, the way you maintain form and look the arrow home after it has sprung from the bow. Soon I'd worn a path from the back deck to the target. In my dreams, every branch in the forest turned into antlers.

To shoot at 30 yards, I had to improvise. Cranking open the little casement window in my office, standing with my right heel touching the back wall and shooting over my computer just about did it. I noticed that the neighbors stopped inviting us to cookouts. Now it was mid-August. I figured 100 arrows a day would make me lethal by the start of deer season in October.

What I was turning into became clear the morning I scared the bejesus out of the UPS man. By this time I had taken to replicating field conditions as closely as I could for my morning 50. A rickety stool atop the picnic table on the back deck got me near-tree-stand height. I wore my fleece camo parka in 85-degree heat, a full-face Scent-Lok hood, with binoculars and a grunt tube slung around my neck. I was an unlikely centaur: deer slayer above the waist; the white hairy legs, gym shorts, and bedroom slippers of the suburban male below.

UPS drivers witness a wider daily range of aberrant human behavior than your average psych-ward nurse. Weird doesn't particularly faze them. But the eyes of the guy in the brown uniform and clipboard told me that he had never seen anything like the Ninja of North Arlington.

"Okay if I just, uh, leave this one on the front porch?" he asked in the overly friendly voice you use on lost children and muggers. He was holding a tiny box of broadheads and keeping the fence between us in case he had to duck and cover.

The whitetail relies on its keen sense of smell, along with its excellent hearing and sight, to detect predators. (Photograph © Stephen Kirkpatrick)

Above: *Whitetail movement occurs most extensively during the autumn months, when rutting bucks are incessantly searching for does. (Photograph © Alan and Sandy Carey)*
Facing page: *If this whitetail buck survives the winter, his polished 5×5 rack will eventually fall off and a new set will sprout in the spring. (Photograph © Mark and Jennifer Miller Photos)*

At times like this, explanations just make you look crazier. "Sure," I told him. I made a gesture of conciliation with my right hand, which still had a string release on it.

Opening day found me 16 feet up a tree on a ridge overlooking a stream crossing. I was wearing rubber boots, camo everything, a charcoal-activated suit, scent killer, and fall masking scent. As light filled the woods, I rattled hard for 30 seconds and watched as a doe and still-dappled fawn came running to see who was new to the neighborhood. She sniffed and stomped. Something was off; she just couldn't tell what. My heart was trying to jackhammer its way out of my chest.

Two weeks later a spike buck came in to the same sound and was actually sniffing at the doe-in-estrus

scent on the boot pads I'd left on a screw-in step. What I didn't have was a shot. I waited, my heart again trying to make a prison break. The deer drifted away, taking the woodiest possible route. At 20 yards he turned his shoulder, and I let one go. The arrow clattered harmlessly against the limbs I hadn't seen, and he trotted off to another appointment. I was disconsolate for days.

Then my hot spot turned cold. Despair made me reckless. I rattled, grunted, and bleated to excess. I lit deer-luring incense sticks and watched them turn to ash. I sprinkled Deer CoCain on the ground. I wondered briefly about real cocaine. I bought several rounds of doe-in-estrus pee for every buck in the house. No gimmick was too stupid for me to buy. If

someone had marketed an Ole Buckster Fart Tube, I'd have ordered two. Some nights back home I'd set up candles by my target and fling arrows out of my office while the rest of the world slept.

The strain was beginning to show in the blue hollows under my eyes. My wife held my hands in her lap one night. "You're sick," Jane said tenderly.

"I know," I replied.

I moved my stand to a trail intersection deeper in the woods. I bought a second stand and put it up along a small bench on a gentle hillside. Forget those articles about how a fixed stand can be set up quietly in 20 minutes and hunted the same day. My personal best was 90 minutes. And it sounded like a Bon Jovi concert.

Thirty of the 40 days of bow season were now gone. I bit the bullet and moved my stands again. I chained one 20 yards in from a fenceline at a crossing where I'd found tiny tufts of hair on the top wire. The other I relocated off to one side of a saddle between my original ridge and its brother.

The dawns and dusks were getting colder. Four days before the end of the season, I spied at a great distance a doe scampering through the leaves. A larger shape, with its head lowered, was tailing her. There was a moment when something that looked like antler caught the slanting afternoon light, but I couldn't be sure.

On the last day of the season, I got to my saddle stand at 2 P.M., climbed up, clipped in, and slowly pulled my bow up. My heart wasn't in it, but I knew I'd kick myself for the rest of the year if I didn't finish it out.

I grunted and rattled. About three-thirty, the deer began to appear. A doe came cautiously into view, so well camouflaged that if I took my eyes off her for a moment, I wouldn't be able to find her again until she moved. Two more does came straight up the saddle, trailed by a 4-pointer with his head down. My heart dropped the clutch and floored it. They were 40 yards out. I rose slowly to my feet, and my stand squeaked. The deer snorted, stomped, and jumped three long lengths away, then stood. I concentrated on taking fast shallow breaths and didn't look directly at them.

The first doe began feeding again. Then another buck, this one sporting 5 points, appeared and began trailing her downwind. They did figure eights through the trees for 45 minutes. As dusk fell, she led him toward my tree. I drew and held. A minute later he turned broadside. I put my pin on his shoulder and released.

The two deer jumped once, then trotted off into the dark woods. I heard hooves clatter on stone. I waited 15 minutes, climbed down with a flashlight in my mouth, and found my bloody arrow nine steps from the base of the tree. Thirty yards away, where I'd heard the clatter, lay the 5-point buck. It took me an hour to drag him 40 yards.

The guy at the slaughterhouse guessed his weight at 180. "That's a big buck," he said.

It occurred to me that I'd shot 6,000 arrows to hear that one sentence. It was worth it.

The thick neck of this whitetail buck is swollen by hormones from the rut. (Photograph © Rich Kirchner/The Green Agency)

GHOST BEARS

by J. B. Stearns

J. B. Stearns was once a successful business consultant. Before that he was an educator, teaching at the private, secondary, and university levels. Before that he took his master's degree in drama and worked as an actor, director, designer, and award-winning playwright. Before that he earned his bachelor's degree in zoology, and before that he was a combat instructor in the Air Force.

Talented in any area at which he chooses to direct his efforts, Stearns has now blessed the world of hunting literature. He is currently a full-time writer with a co-authored book on his native Vermont and articles in outdoors magazines such as *Game Journal* and *Shooting Sportsman*. The following story, which originally appeared in the May 1997 issue of *Gray's Sporting Journal,* details the physical effort and mental determination necessary to pack a sodden black bear out of the Vermont woods.

My godfather had bears all over the place. Polar bears, grizzly bears, kodiak bears and a squadron of Vermont black bears. Grinning bears, smiling bears and, from less imaginative taxidermists, just plain sanguine bears. Bear rugs with mounted heads and feet draped the great curving banisters of Linden Terrace's sweeping central staircase and lolled before its fireplaces. As a child I'd loved those bears, rolled on them, stared at them for hours.

I was deer hunting, not bear hunting, but the seasons overlap, and the disturbance in the snow definitely was a fresh bear print. Well, you can eat a bear as well as you can eat a deer; you just have to cook the meat longer if you don't want little worms crawling around in your muscles. And I *wanted* one of those fierce bear rugs of my childhood. So, suddenly, I was bear hunting.

I was about a mile beyond the end of Willis Cemetery Road, heading toward Somerset Reservoir, when I picked up his prints. A tracking snow had fallen the night before, and the temperature held below freezing. The prints were deep and all but steaming, evenly spaced and meandering a bit. This bear was in no hurry. His trail veered toward several large beech trees, where pawed circles in the snow told of his taste for beechnuts. The slight breeze was in my face. The black wasn't worried about his back trail. As long as he stayed hungry and calm, I had a chance of running up on him without his knowing—long enough for one shot, maybe. If he discovered me following him, somebody else might get a chance, but he'd never let me close enough to see him.

The forest-dwelling black bear is North America's most common and widespread bear. This Alaskan bear is one of hundreds of thousands of black bears that live throughout the continent. (Photograph © Tom Walker)

Above: *The name "black bear" is a misnomer, for the animal's color phases include shades of brown, beige-blonde, and even a blue-white color. This Montanan black bear is in its cinnamon phase. (Photograph © Art Wolfe)*
Facing page: *Inland black bears tend to have brown coats, while bears that live in coastal areas with high rainfall usually have black fur. This dark-coated black bear was photographed on a tidal flat in coastal Alaska. (Photograph © Daniel J. Cox/Natural Exposures Inc.)*

Although Vermont has a high density of black bears, ever since bear trapping was outlawed most kills have come from opportunistic deer hunters, a few trained packs of bear dogs and baiting. And while the Fish and Game Department takes a dim view of the latter activity, it isn't unusual to see the limbs of bygone apple orchards in the Northeast Kingdom hung with weighted gunnysacks. What weights them depends on a particular outlaw's family formula. Some hold with guts, some with fruit pulp, others with mixtures as complex and outlandish as a witch's brew.

Legal hunters tend to stake out old home orchards near empty cellar holes, where trees still hang with wormy fruit and show fresh claw marks on their shaggy trunks and where the swale between trees is beaten down in vomit-marked paths. Today's hunters don't chase down their quarry. I've read of the old-timers doing it, but we have neither their stamina nor their woods sense. And matched against a bear's nose, ears and running gear? Well, it's like a junior-high pick-up team playing the Harlem Globe Trotters.

The bear passed out of the mixed woods where I had picked up his track and started beelining through a clear-cut section growing up to dense, head-high spruce. Once into this I immediately lost the trail. I couldn't even see the ground, but there was no tracking snow on it anyway. The young trees were so closely interlocked that all the snow was in their branches. Just blindly bulling through the mess meant snow in the face, snow up the armholes, snow down the neck. But something in us senses patterns, and 20 minutes later, when I broke free of the spruce, I was nearly on the bear's tracks. Maybe the bear

knocked enough snow off the trees to provide a path that I unconsciously followed, or perhaps we both just followed the path of least resistance.

I believed I knew where he was heading. Bordering the east side of Somerset Reservoir are two large swamps divided by a ribbon of high ground running right to the lake. I quickly made for that ridge, trying to keep the tracks in view, but as I made the high ground I realized I'd lost them. I wasn't even sure where I'd last seen them.

I stood slack-jawed, cursing myself for a fool. I'd have to backtrack to where I'd left the bear's trail, which might mean I'd never catch up with him. And with the day wearing, time was against me.

So often hunting success has as much to do with luck as with guile and skill. I heard thrashing to my left followed by the outraged *woooeeeks* of wood ducks, and through the leafless snags I saw the bear 150 yards out in the swamp. I dropped to a sitting position, wound my scope down to 2X and tried to find the bear. That's never as easy for me as it seems to be for everyone else. But I did find him, screwed the scope to 10, lost him, went back to 5, found him plowing slowly through the swamp again, pushed off the safety, held for a heart shot, held my breath and tried to squeeze evenly. The bear staggered but didn't fall. I panicked and, about as quickly as I could have fired an autoloader, bolted two more shots. The bear splashed and I jumped up, peering through my scope to make sure it hadn't gotten a second life. Then it hit me: I'd just dropped a very large bear in the middle of a very wet and snag-ridden swamp. The next part of this little adventure would not be as much fun as the first.

There was no best way. I tried hummock hopping, but by the fifth hummock, I was in to the knees, my boots filling with ooze. A third of the way there I fully realized that I was facing one hell of a job getting that bear back to solid ground, assuming I actually made it to the bear.

When I got there, sweating, wheezing, legs barked and skinned by stumps and snags, I found a big bear, a heavy bear and, on one side, a soaking-wet bear. With a vague idea that I wanted to keep his front end up as I dragged, I made a shoulder harness out of the rope I always carry when hunting and tied the bear's front paws to his neck on either side of his head. At first I tried to drag cleverly, but there's no clever way to haul such a load through a swamp. I was reduced to the brute force of the berserker. Slogging, wailing, crawling through a mucky, ice-skimmed landscape, levering from the backside of hummocks, clawing at anything solid enough to pull on. Bears do not pull easily, I learned. They catch on things, everything, and they are ungodly flexible.

An extended temper tantrum finally got us to firm ground, where I'd left my rifle and hunting coat. I was spent, soggy and filthy to the chest. My hands shook as I gutted the bear on the clean snow. It was getting late, and with miles to go I didn't dare rest. Gutted, the bear would be lighter, I told myself.

It was nearing sunset when I finished. It was too far to go back the way I'd come, but if I followed the lake north then struck straight north off its end, I'd eventually come out on the Kelly Stand Road. Not much traffic, but during deer season there'd be some, enough to get a ride back to Willis Cemetery. I started off. A dead bear doesn't sledge across the top of the earth as a dead deer does. A bear melds, flows and swaggles into every hole and divot and unevenness of the ground, clutching and sucking at them. Bear-pulling over rough ground is even worse than bear-pulling in swamps.

I was wet and evaporating, my legs quaking like aspens in the wind. I wouldn't have made it out that night even if the river hadn't gotten in my way. I should have known there was a river there; something had to fill the lake. It wasn't a big river as rivers go, but it was big enough, fast enough, deep enough and cut through enough of a ravine to settle the matter. I stopped pulling and started gathering firewood and building a pine- and spruce-bough lean-to on the high bank.

My arms and shoulders felt like lead, except lead doesn't hurt, and I hurt everywhere. And I was cold right through to my spinal cord, roaring fire notwithstanding. A breeze was up, and the forest moaned with the unearthly sound of tree limbs rubbing, rubbing—spirit music, the old-timers called it.

The black bear is the one member of the family Ursidae *that has a great capacity to live in close proximity to humans, although—like any wild animal—it will respond to human approach. (Photograph © D. R. Fernandez and M. L. Peck)*

This Michigan black bear may gain as much as thirty pounds per week in the fall, foraging constantly in response to its instinctual drive to bulk up before winter hibernation. (Photograph © Alan and Sandy Carey)

I fell asleep with that thought and awoke in the middle of a dream. I had been painting the inside of my garage with the door open, heard a grunt behind me and spun around to see beady black eyes and a long black snout: a bear standing two feet away, staring. I smacked him across the nose with my wet paint brush; he roared and reared, and I snapped awake.

For a few minutes I couldn't move, and then I eased up and threw kindling on the ruby coals and dragged over more dead branches. As I lay back down, my back felt like a thick slab of ice. I thought of a mastodon on its back, slowly thawing from a glacier. I rolled away from the new blaze and slept again.

Pre-dawn came cold and early. The fire was dead, and I was numb and stiff. I danced around to get the heat pumps going and started wrenching dead branches from pine trees.

With a new blaze going, my thoughts turned to food—mastodon steaks, hanging from forked sticks

before my fire. Bear steaks were out. Bear meat must be well cooked, and I don't know anyone who can cook a bear steak trichinae-killing-done in front of a bonfire without burning it beyond recognition. Besides, how do you drag a filleted bear? I looked at the bear instead.

It was beautiful, gleaming like a midnight apparition. I resolved to use every bit of it: the meat, the hide, the paws, even the bones. We'd always done that with whatever we raised or shot around the Vermont hill farm where I grew up. "Waste not, want not," my father said. He was full of aphorisms. "Use it up, wear it out, make it do or do without." Whenever Mother jawed at him, he'd recite them, one after another, on and on, until she nearly exploded.

Of course, I still had to get the bear back. The river was raging from fall rain and melting snow, and I wanted desperately to stay dry. I walked upstream to see if things got better. They didn't, but I found a large tree fallen across the head of a big pool at the bottom of a falls. I could get across on that, I thought, but not carrying a bear.

I don't know why leaving the bear and going for help was out of the question, but it was. Not that I was afraid someone would steal my meat; few hunters came in this deep. I guess in a way it was because I loved that bear. I'd started talking to it while cleaning it, encouraged it to come along on the haul to the stream, chatted to it by the fire last night. We'd become friends, the bear and I, and you can't leave a friend in the woods. And I had an idea.

I returned to camp, buried my fire and tobogganed the bear to the stub of the cross-stream tree, a thumping big oak. I untied the shoulder-harness end of the rope and rolled the bear off the edge of the cut. He crashed down and came to rest at the water's edge. I tied the other end of the rope to my belt and shinnied across the log. I ran out of rope before reaching the bank and had to slide down to the wa-

ter. I put all my weight on the rope, and the bear eased into the water, hung briefly on some rocks and then entered the flood. I wound the rope around my arms and hung on, and the bear arced beautifully across the torrent and swept up on a sloping rock shelf at the bottom of the pool. What had seemed the most difficult problem in this ordeal turned out to be the easiest.

Getting the bear up the steep bank was another matter. The last four feet were nearly vertical. I'd reach that point and run out of strength, and the bear would slip back. I'd rest and pull again with the same results, only each time I'd feel weaker.

All that work, all that pain, and I was going to lose it. I *wanted* that chunk of my childhood. I wanted one of those Linden Terrace bears. Then I went berserk again, screaming profanities and raging that thing up out of the ravine.

The rest of the drag was reasonably level and unevent-

Black bear make their home in the coniferous forests of the West and Midwest and the hardwood forests of the East. They prefer dense woods that provide protective undergrowth. (Photograph © Bill McRae)

ful. Just never-ending brush, sags, gullies, rocks and snags. I thought of other bears I'd known: the one on upper Turkey Mountain brook with a brook-trout tail sticking out from his chicken lips; the one that taunted my neighbor, Freeman Hollis, who sat evening after evening, for weeks, in an abandoned orchard, waiting for a bear that came only at night. Freeman said that after he'd gone back to his car and driven to the top of the gap road and stopped to hear the night, he'd hear that damn bear bawling. He thought it was laughing.

I started talking to the bear again. I told him the story of how old E.N. Woodcock, down in Pennsylvania in the Kinzua, had trailed a bear dragging a trap through four counties for six days. He—and the bear, too, he supposed—simply stopped and slept on the trail when night overtook them.

"I guess you could have done that as well as an 1870s bear," I told it. "But I couldn't. Those old long-line trappers were tougher than old rooster meat. Bears may be as good as they ever were, but hunters aren't. I couldn't take six days of this even if I weren't dragging you."

Then late in the afternoon, I found myself on the edge of the Kelly Stand Road. I gave a mental whoop, babbled a bit more to the bear, then lay down beside the narrow dirt road with my head on the bear's neck and went to sleep. Eventually a road hunter was bound to come along, and we'd catch a ride back to Willis Cemetery.

At dusk I became aware of two faces—slightly incredulous, slightly afraid—peering from a rusty Chevy Suburban with Connecticut tags. I got up. "Can you give us a lift down to Willis Cemetery Road?"

"We thought you were dead," said one of the mouths.

"Nope. Only the bear. Can you give us a lift?"

"Sure." They loaded the bear into the back of the Suburban.

"God, he's a big one," one said.

"Yeah," said the other. "Look at those claws—and choppers," he added, skinning back the bear's upper lip. "Where'd you get him?"

"Over to Somerset—yesterday afternoon." I couldn't resist a bit of pride. Give these guys something to tell their friends back in suburbia. The in-

side of the Suburban was warm, almost hot. It felt good.

"Hot damn. That must've been one helluva drag. Fur got kind of banged up towards the rear end there, didn't it? We're from near Norwalk." The driver kept talking, and I started to doze off.

I'm going to use every bit of that bear, I thought. Chops, roasts, steaks, boot grease, a rug with head and claws. Just like at Linden Terrace.

The Roman-nosed profile of this black bear distinguishes it from the grizzly, which possesses a more concave, dished face. (Photograph © Stephen Kirkpatrick)

Chapter 5

❖————◆————❖

THE HUNTING EXPERIENCE

"The slow, steady flow of events and impressions—the fecund smell of spring in the countryside, the jazzy trill of red-winged blackbirds, heart-shaped prints in the dust, a warm afternoon zephyr rattling through the cottonwoods—these things, singly and together, were every bit as meaningful as contact with game."
—David Petersen, "Mentors," 1998

EXCERPT FROM
HEART AND BLOOD

by Richard Nelson

The traditional climax of a hunting tale is the kill, the point at which the hunter attains the quarry. But many hunters know that any hunt goes beyond that moment of contact. Richard Nelson is one of those sage persons.

Nelson, at the age of twenty-two, was offered the opportunity to live with the Inuit of Alaska's Arctic coast and study their hunting traditions. This undertaking led to the publication of his first book, *Hunters of the Northern Ice* (1969), a collection of ethnographic material on the Inuit of Wainwright village. His experiences with the Inuit fueled a lifelong desire to study traditional cultures, learn from their ways, and spread the wisdom inherent in their lifestyle. He explains that his attraction to subsistence hunters stems from their intimate connection with their surrounding natural environment. Perhaps most influential to Nelson have been the Koyukon Athabaskan of Alaska's interior, with "their teachings about respectful behavior toward nature."

The following story is excerpted from his 1997 book, *Heart and Blood*, an elegant exploration of America's relationship with the deer that live within its boundaries. In the book, Nelson hunts blacktailed deer amidst a rainstorm raging on an Alaskan island—a sensuous experience that makes his hunt much more than the successful taking of game.

Awake in my sleeping bag, I stare into the black fissure of night, listening to raindrops flail against the cabin roof, gusts hiss in the treetops, waves pound on the nearby rocks. I reassure myself that the skiff is securely anchored and tethered by a safety line to a tree on shore. At last, in the dim light before dawn, I can see the boat still nested in our sheltered cove. Haida Strait, on the other hand, is a pandemonium of whitecaps, with thick-bellied swells pouring across submerged reefs and detonating against bare islets.

Half a mile offshore, there's a flock of several hundred gulls, circling and undulating like mist in a cataract. What inspires these birds to seek out the storm instead of heading for a protected bay? Do the frothing waves stir up food? Or do gulls simply love riding the wind, as I would if I had wings? Never mind such questions, I tell myself: the searing, storm-sung enchantment of the sky is reason enough.

Obviously, Keta and I won't be going home this afternoon as planned. Through a spatter of raindrops on the window, I peer into the gloom, watching black water tremble in the cove. I could fire up the woodstove and hunker inside, since most of the deer will bed in thickets until the wind and rain diminish, but I can't resist the temptation to head outside, drawn by an urge to stalk through the woods and muskegs, and to feel the storm's onrushing power. A full suit of rain gear might seem perfect on a day like this, but wearing nylon or some other noisy outfit makes it almost impossible to approach wildlife. Instead, I'll wear my usual outfit—wool jacket and polypropylene pants—soft, quiet clothes that keep you fairly warm even when they're soaked.

Keta and I trudge up the long, wooded slope behind Bear Cove, and by the time we reach open muskeg there's sweat on my brow. From then on we set a slower pace, staying near the muskeg's fringe, where forest creates a sheltered lee and deer might abandon cover to feed. Although it's quieter here, the wind and rain make enough noise to help mask our sloshy footsteps.

Everything around us is alive with raindrops—dappling tea-colored ponds, shimmering on gray trunks, clinging to needles and boughs, hanging from cottongrass fluff and withered shooting stars, splashing on mushroom crowns and bog cranberries, running down salmonberry leaves and blades of grass, soaking into sedges, saturating the soil, trickling down rivulets and streams.

Half a mile into the muskeg, Keta starts lifting her snout and peering ahead. I'm sure she's caught a rich blacktail scent . . . but has the deer already detected our approach? In hunting or watching wild animals, it's crucial to remember we carry around us a shifting halo of scent that drifts on the breeze, stretches into threads and plumes, gathers in pools and eddies, and flows off into the distance—totally beyond our own senses but unmistakable to deer. At the same time, we produce a halo of sound in the pattern of our footsteps, breaths, and scrapes against vegetation; and we create a visual halo that betrays us at ranges varying with cover, light, and terrain.

I try to imagine how far and in what direction our halos disperse, while I stay alert for the muted halos of sound and sight also given off by deer; and at the same time I watch Keta to borrow acuteness from her senses. Both the deer and I strive to conceal ourselves, as we also try to break through the other's concealment. For countless millennia, hunters and prey have carried out this complex interweaving of mind and senses; it lies at the core of our existence; it braids our separate lives together.

Keta's eagerness heightens as we track slowly upwind, immersed in a dense streamer of scent. Finally she hesitates, stiffens, and stares intently. Kneeling beside her, following her gaze, I eventually pick out a doe—smaller than I would hunt—almost perfectly camouflaged amid a backdrop of tawny beige grass, dusky tree trunks, and whirling rain. A prolonged standoff ensues, the deer absolutely motionless while I struggle to keep almost as still. For 15 minutes she never stirs, never unfastens her eyes, never so much as twitches an ear, until I can't help feeling perplexed and wonder if she'll ever turn us loose. It's as if time moves differently in our two minds, as if this extended wait is nothing but a moment—or nothing in the world at all—for the deer.

When I glance away and then look back, the doe seems to have dissolved; but then, meticulously searching the spot, I discover she's still there, half lost in the mysterious perceptual veil that always seems to surround deer, the marvelously perfected cryptogram shaped by a million years of evolution. Deer are not *supposed* to be seen by predators, after all.

At last the doe breaks our impasse, reaches down to nibble a wet petal, flicks the raindrops from her

The stocky mule deer, named for its long mulelike ears, evolved across the West in a varied terrain of badlands, plains, deserts, and mountains. (Photograph © Bill McRae)

A cowbird perches on the head of an Oregon blacktail buck in velvet. (Photograph © Curt Given)

tail, and struts away in an exaggerated gait reminiscent of a prancing show horse, forelegs raised high and bent elegantly above her hooves, as if to render me harmless at the sight of her unalloyed beauty. Then she bursts into a four-footed trampoline stott, hesitates once to glance back at us, and flounces off like tumbling water. I watch her vanish into the forest, rain flowing like a river in my eyes.

In the hours that follow, Keta and I drift along the muskeg's border without coming across another blacktail. Keta's soaked, clinging coat makes her look skinny and a bit wretched, although she's as lively and wagtailed as ever. My clothes are totally waterlogged, but I'm still fairly warm, thanks to steady trekking and southerly gales bringing temperatures well up into the forties. Despite the pleasure and excitement of rambling around in a storm, I also feel a growing urgency about the hunt. We're short of camp food, so we must head back tomorrow if the wind subsides. At home, last year's venison is about gone, and this is the ideal season for replenishing

our supply—a time when bucks, especially, have reached maximum size and prime condition just before the rut.

Around midafternoon I abandon the muskeg and work along a narrow peninsula of forest with a deeply incised creek rushing through the middle. Here, during a long session with the call, a small, spike-antlered buck emerges from the underbrush, eases in our direction, head high and ears wide, but then flashes away—as if the wind has made him frazzled and hypersensitive.

A bit farther on, we come across a thick cedar tree with long pieces of bark peeled off, as you might tear vertical bands of tape from a wall. Some lie coiled like wet pythons beneath the tree, but others are still attached 15 feet above the ground, hanging loosely over the smooth, shiny wood. Undamaged bark covers about half the trunk and the tree looks healthy, although it's too soon to know if it will survive. A wildlife biologist told me that brown bears sometimes pull off cedar bark this way in springtime, then lick the heavy-flowing sap either for a tasty treat or a nutritional boost.

Closer inspection of this tree reveals faint tooth marks, some well above my head, and the surrounding earth is worn raw, indicating the bear stayed here for a while, scraping and rolling and scuffling. Although there is nothing subtle or inconspicuous about these workings, and although I must have passed many trees like this over the years, I never noticed them until I'd talked with the biologist. It's often like this, I think: we're blind to much of the world until someone tells us how to see it.

The storm shows no sign of relenting as afternoon gives way to evening. From a ridgetop, I look out over Haida Strait—still a torrent of whitecaps, the offshore islets half lost in rain squalls, thick stratus surging overhead. I turn my face toward the sky, let the raindrops prickle my skin, and feel grateful to be alive in this saturated kingdom of clouds. After months of tranquil weather, the whole world seems caught up in a boisterous celebration, as if the season isn't just turning, it's doing handsprings. I'm exalted by the wildness of it all, ready for the cold and fire and passion of winter.

At times the gale blows so hard that the rhythm of my tired footsteps seems almost inconsequential, but I still try to keep quiet, staying on the highest, least spongy ground as we trek along the muskeg's edge. Little time remains before nightfall, so there's not much chance we'll come across any more deer. And yet, judging by the abundance of tracks, droppings, and clipped vegetation, more than one blacktail would hear the sound if I clapped my hands.

All around us is lovely parklike heath scattered with bonsai-sized pines, veiled in mist and rain. It's as if everything had been set perfectly in place, according to some meticulous yet whimsical design, and even I—a man freshly rooted here—feel myself a part of it, a single voice in a deafeningly beautiful chorus. I am an *animal,* moving among other animals, surrounded by plants, wrapped in a cloak of rain, breathing wind, feet sunken into the moss, the great earth plunging away below.

With the approach of dusk, I have no choice but to head back toward the cove. We haven't come across fresh bear signs today, but I'm still jittery from last evening's experience and don't care to grope through the woods in darkness. Retracing our earlier route,

Keta and I approach the spot where we saw the first doe this morning. It's fairly calm and quiet under the leaning brow of trees, so I move along slowly and pause every few steps to look around . . . but just ahead is a broad, open meadow—not the sort of place where I'd expect to see deer, especially during a storm.

Keta grabs a stick and begs me to play, but I motion her to settle down; if nothing else, stepping along carefully and silently will keep my senses alert, heightening my awareness of the wind, the rain, and the softly dwindling light. I pick my way through a patch of deer cabbage, then look up to scan the area ahead.

In that fraction of a second, everything is changed, and I catch myself in midstep as the truth of it bolts through me. At the same instant, Keta sags into a half crouch, her neck leaning forward, her ears honed and eyes riveted, her legs quivering, one forepaw lifted off the ground.

There, standing atop a low rise about 20 yards ahead, silhouetted above the crowns of two stunted pines, hard edged against the faded, hoary overcast, are the chest and neck and head of a deer, faced directly toward us, eyes shining, ears in a wide V, and a beamy crescent of antlers bending above.

Without hesitating and without conscious thought, I sink onto my knees, raise the rifle to my shoulder, and brace it against a slender tree. During these seconds, I'm taken by a powerful sense of déjà vu. At this same season a few years ago, a buck stood against the evening sky less than a hundred yards from this spot, and I did exactly what I'm doing now.

Perhaps this is why the outcome seems just as certain. There is no tingling apprehension, no pounding heart, no shaking hand. The rifle sights come to rest, unwavering. I breathe deeply, and deeply again, eyes opened wide. It's as if everything were preordained and the animal had come—as Koyukon elders teach—to give itself.

I feel absolutely, jarringly predatory, like a cat splayed against the grass, simmering in ambush. And utterly alive, in a way that defies language, that scarcely renders itself in conscious thought. I am a living creature questing for its food. Whatever ambiguity I feel about the hunt, it now lies far beyond reach. And I say this: No tiller of soil, no herder of flocks, no gatherer of plants, no browser of grocery shelves will ever cross this same emotional terrain. As for me, I would rather be a rock on a hillside than exist without knowing in this way the animal who lives inside me and gives me life.

The buck pumps his head up and down, telegraphing his uncertainty. Then he stands utterly still, his shape incised above the curving cloud of branches, as if the full truth of him had leapt down into the fluid of my eye.

Lightning flashes brightly in the blackness, and thunder pours away over the land's edge, tumbling and tumbling beneath the storm.

There is a burst and a shock and a jarred half vision of the deer's fall, as if he were completely released, like a puppet whose strings have all been snipped at once. I stand, breathing heavily, and rush toward the empty place between the pines with Keta bounding alongside. She reaches the spot before me, circles, and snuffles the soft edges of the buck. He lies on a mat of crowberry and bog laurel, soft and quiet and midnight-still—as if the gale had instantly grown calm.

At first I hear only silence. Then I hear my heart pounding and the ringing in my ears, and finally Keta panting at my side, the swashing of wind in high boughs, the distant drum of surf.

I kneel beside the deer and touch his warm, silky eye to affirm the certainty of death. Then I run my hand along his flank, whispering words of thanks that seem inadequate and frail against what I've been given here—a life that will enter and sustain my own. Beaded raindrops roll down over the dry, brittle fur.

I am not a guiltless hunter, but neither do I hunt without joy. What fills me now is an incongruous mix of grief and satisfaction, excitement and calm, humility and pride. And the recognition that death is the rain that fills the river of life inside us all.

Keta prances back and forth excitedly, looking in all directions for another deer, as if animals fascinate her only when they're running or might do so. I hold her by my side, rub her fur, and nuzzle her wet face. The deer is a prime, heavy, thick-coated buck, bearing modest but lovely antlers, their slender beams stained dark maroon at the base, fading to polished gray on each of the six elegantly tapered points. I will leave them here, although it's not hard to understand why someone might hang them on a living-room wall.

After dragging the buck to a nearby tree, I fasten a rope around both forelegs, loop it over a branch, then hoist the animal off the ground. With a small pocket knife, I sever the neck and spinal cord, then make a shallow incision, slightly longer than my hand, down the middle of the deer's belly, being careful not to puncture its stomach, which would foul the body cavity with spilled contents. Next I reach up into the hot, moist cavity to pull out the stomach, intestines, and fatty mesenteries, leaving the heart, liver, and kidneys in place. Keta nudges close, trying to lick the blood that drips down, but I shoo her away out of respect for the animal. Later on, when we butcher the deer, Keta will have her share of scraps.

I take some fat from inside the body, plus a few slivers of meat, and leave them with the viscera for the other animals. It's important, Koyukon people say, that wild creatures feed on remnants left in the woods by hunters, but other than small tidbits, nothing should be abandoned except parts we can't use ourselves. The eagles and ravens will come at first light tomorrow and within an hour they'll clean up everything but the skull bones and stomach contents.

To make sure no dirt gets inside the carcass, I cut small holes through the skin around the belly and neck openings, then lace them shut with cord. Next, I half sever the forelegs at their "knee" joints and toggle each front leg through a sliced opening in the hock of the corresponding rear leg. This makes it possible to carry a modest-sized deer as if it were a pack, putting your arms through the fastened legs and hoisting it up so the animal's belly lies against your back. With darkness looming above mountains to the east, I start the final trudge. Keta dances alongside, perhaps anticipating tonight's dinner. I'll cut a few pieces of fresh venison to fry in a skillet atop the wood-burning stove—the most delicious and elemen-

Facing page: *This muley buck has recently shed its velvet, as revealed by its blood-stained antlers and fuzzy strips trailing down its neck. (Photograph © Erwin and Peggy Bauer)*
Overleaf: *After the velvet on this muley buck's rack is rubbed off, its long antlers will be left hard and ready for sparring. (Photograph © Len Rue Jr.)*

tal feast I can imagine, making the deer a part of me.

In the last stretch of muskeg, just before we'll enter the woods behind Bear Cove, I angle over to a small, rain-dappled lake, put my load on the ground, and rest beside the water. Keta slumps against me, finally getting tired. But she perks up a few minutes later, when a large doe ghosts out from the trees directly across the lake from us and steps to the water's edge, nervously switching her tail. She reaches down and touches her nose to the water . . . and it's as if I have drifted into a deer's dream.

I slowly bend over, dip my hand beneath the ripples, and fill it with the same chill water. And there, embraced by the island and the sky, we drink each other down.

Mule deer are most comfortable in open wooded mountain and foothill areas. These muley bucks live in California's Tule Lake National Wildlife Region. (Photograph © Jeffrey Rich)

LITTLE BENNY'S RUG

by Glenn Balch

Born in 1902 and educated in Texas, a graduate student at Columbia University in New York City, and stationed variously in India, Burma, and China during World War II, Glenn Balch always returned to his chosen home—the mountains of Idaho. Two winters spent snowbound in central Idaho's remote Sawtooth Mountains offered the seclusion necessary to begin a writing career, and in 1931, Balch quit the *Idaho Daily Statesman* to devote himself full-time to freelance writing.

With over thirty published books, including a multitude of beloved children's books, four nonfiction horse guides, and two Western novels, Balch is recognized as Idaho's most published writer. Best known as the author of the popular "Tack Ranch" children's series, Balch was also a regular contributor to outdoors magazines such as *Field & Stream*, where the following story appeared in 1934. One of America's original Western writers, Balch brings us a tale replete with the many-faceted pleasures of hunting—including relinquishing the kill for a different kind of satisfaction.

T he other day a mountain man brought me down a pure-white goat-skin rug, expertly cured and as soft and fluffy as it is possible for a goat skin to be. I packed it carefully for shipment and sent it to an address in Philadelphia. I didn't kill that goat, and I don't know the person to whom I sent the hide; but when the package had disappeared through the parcel-post window, insured far above its actual value, I had a feeling of pride and satisfaction in a job well done. And thereby hangs a tale.

It is a tale of Dad Lightfoot, my old mountaineer pal who has lived for nearly half a century in the big central Idaho wilderness. Dad surprised me by appearing in Boise one day last fall.

"You dog-goned old scalawag!" I greeted him affectionately, aware that the grip of his hard-knuckled brown old hand was paralyzing my arm from the elbow down. "What the devil are you doing here? Gosh, but I'm glad to see you!"

"Howdy, son." Dad usually addresses me that way, although we are not related except by a mutual love of the outdoors. "I'm in a jack-pot, an' you can help me out."

"Not the cops?" I asked, recalling a time when the old mountaineer's contempt for man-made laws had landed him in the hoosegow. It was there that I, news-hawking, met him and won his friendship by bridging the gap between his obstinacy and the police captain's forgiveness.

The mountain goat, native to the mountains of northwest North America, is considered a goat antelope.
(Photograph © John W. Herbst)

Dad chuckled indulgently. "Rub it in," he invited. "But it's somethin' else this time—somethin' much more important."

This mountain man has one of the most engaging personalities that I have ever come in contact with. The magnetism lies in his eyes. They are so startlingly clear and honest, so powerfully clean and capable and independent. They have a way of gazing into the far-off distances as if overlooking the trivial disappointments close at hand for the more important goal of a life well lived. This philosophy comes from close and intimate contact with nature, from a minimum of the worries and troubles that civilization strews in the path of us luxury chasers, and, perhaps most of all, from the gratification of a life lived in freedom of all but nature's laws.

Somehow I feel that Dad's scheme of things is the true life, the happy life; and that the rest of us are by our very struggles robbing ourselves of much that we struggle for. A superfluity of ambition, copybooks to the contrary notwithstanding, may be the reason for it.

"Come into the hotel," I said, taking his arm and steering him through the big swinging doors. "I'll buy you a glass of something zippy and a good cigar. Then you can tell me all about it."

"Good water—spring water if they've got it—is what I want," the old man declared. "An'," reaching into his pocket for his stubby old pipe, "I'll take a tin o' plug slice instead o' that seegar."

"Now," I said, after we were comfortably seated and Dad had his pipe going, "what's the trouble?"

The old fellow chuckled with mystifying satisfaction. "It ain't exactly trouble," he said. "It's a new arrival in the family."

"What!" I snorted. "Why, you old skinflint, you!"

"Hold yore hosses a minute," Dad interrupted. "Don't get me wrong. It's my niece's family. She lives back in Philadelphy."

"And how does that get you in trouble?" I asked. The old man pulled a dirty envelope from his pocket and waved it jubilantly in my face.

"They named it Benjamin, after me," he said ex-

This billy's shaggy winter coat shows off the mountain goat's distinctive crest of long, erect hair along the neck, shoulders, and spine. (Photograph © John W. Herbst)

citedly, his bronzed countenance shining with delight.

"Well," I asked, "what are you going to do about it?"

"That's what I want to know," he said. "What ought I to do about it? What's the proper thing? A man has got to do the proper thing when he becomes a godfather, ain't he?"

"Oh, so that's what's worrying you," I said, beginning to understand. "Why, just send your niece your congratulations, and little Benny a present."

"Golly, that's a relief," Dad said. "Now," he went on, "what are we goin' to get him?"

"We?" I raised my eyebrows.

"Yes, we!" he declared with emphasis on the pronoun. "I ain't wet-nursed you on big-game hunts an' cooked for you an' washed dishes after you for nothin', by gosh! You can't run out on me when I'm in a jam. You've got to see me through this thing."

I stared at the old man and saw that he was in dead earnest.

"Sure, Dad," I promised solemnly, "I'll stick by you."

"All right, then. The big question is, what are we goin' to get him?"

Suddenly I had an idea, a peach of an idea—one of the kind that kills two birds with one stone.

"A goat-skin rug," I said. "It's just the thing. Can't you just see the little cuss wallowing on a pure-white goat-skin rug?"

From the way Dad's eyes shone, I knew he could. "Betcha," he gloated, "no other kid in Philadelphy has got one."

"And I'll come up and kill it for you," I offered magnanimously. That was the second bird.

Old Dad has long since quit hunting, except on those very rare occasions when he gets an appetite for venison, but his clear gray eyes regarded me a little dubiously.

"Can you kill a goat with a metal-jacketed bullet so it won't damage the hide—just one shot, mind you?"

"Can you tan goat so the hair will smell like es-

sence of lilacs and the other side will be a skin you love to touch?" I shot back at him sharply.

The old fellow stuck out his big bone-crushing paw. "It's a bargain," he said. "Get yore gun an' let's go."

By lantern light we saddled a couple of horses in the old pole corral at Dad's place, high in the mountains. I had done considerable hunting from that cabin, but never before with Dad. He always refused to go out with us, saying that he wasn't killing any more game, not for himself or anybody else, unless meat was needed. On this occasion, however, he was influenced by a mighty purpose, and I was thrilled at the prospect of having him along. Dad Lightfoot knows more about those big Idaho crags and the sheep and goats that live in them than any person I have ever met.

By nine o'clock we were climbing the skirts of a great craggy peak that thrust its saffron spirals and towers into the deep blue of the heavens. Dad kept Nell, his old saddle mare, pushing steadily upward through the tall spruce and fir.

"We're goin' to get the biggest dog-gone goat on that mountain," he declared happily. "We're goin' to send a hide back to little Benny that he can be proud of—one so danged big he'll have to roll over three times to get off the edge."

I was all for it. "Just show me the one you want, Dad," I instructed, "and I'll do the rest."

Dad wasn't carrying a gun; but a big hand-forged skinning knife, whetted to a hair-splitting keenness, was sheathed on his belt.

We came upon a black bear clawing a rotted log for grubs. He ambled away with a laughable mixture of dignity and apprehensiveness.

A mile or so farther on, Dad interrupted his low, tuneful whistling to ask me if I would like to see a moose. I replied that I would.

The old mountaineer turned sharply to the right, zigzagged over a low ridge and shortly pulled his horse to a halt in the concealment of an aspen thicket. We had stopped near the shore of a small lake so artfully hidden that one had to be almost in

Facing page: The shaggy "white bear" furs that eighteenth-century British explorer James Cook, the famed "Captain Cook," purchased during his voyages to the Pacific were actually the pelts of mountain goats. (Photograph © D. Robert Franz)
Overleaf: A mountain goat walks a narrow ledge in Southeast Alaska. Although they have adapted to their alpine domain, many goats show healed wounds and missing teeth as a result of falls. (Photograph © Daniel J. Cox/Natural Exposures Inc.)

the water to see it.

"There's Annie an' her young-un'," he informed me in a soft undertone. "I don't see John; guess he's round on the other side o' the point, divin' for lily bulbs."

I peered through the screen and was almost dumfounded by the sight of a great cow moose, closely followed by a calf, feeding leisurely in the shallow water.

"Annie had twins last year," Dad informed me as he backed Nellie around and rode away.

"But I've always been told there weren't any moose in this section," I said.

"Yeah, I've been told that too," Dad replied, spitting contemptuously over an alder shrub.

Near timber-line the old mountaineer pulled his horse to a sudden halt and swung down out of the saddle.

"Bring yore gun," he whispered.

I followed at his heels, marveling that he could move so swiftly and carelessly and yet with so little noise. My own booted feet seemed to crush dry leaves and twigs every time I put them down.

On his belly, Dad wriggled like a snake through a chaparral thicket. The branches scratched at my face and pulled at my clothing, but eventually I reached a place beside him. He was peering cautiously through a thin screen of leaves, and as I paused I saw, through this screen, a dozen or more indistinct white bodies about one hundred and fifty yards away. Goats—mountain goats—as sure as I was alive!

I pulled my rifle hastily forward, thrust the muzzle through the screen and saw clearly, through the opening above the barrel, a big shaggy white form.

"Wait," Dad whispered.

After a long, nerve-racking minute, Dad startled me by speaking aloud.

"Our goat ain't in that bunch, son," he said, getting to his feet.

I got up in time to see the white forms vanish around the base of a cliff, trotting with superb indifference over sloping rock at the edge of a sheer drop of many feet.

"They look plenty good to me," I informed Dad.

He shook his head. "Not good enough for little Benny," he declared.

At timber-line we unsaddled the horses, hobbled them and turned them loose to graze on the rich bunch-grass.

"Never leave a hoss tied if you don't know how long it'll be 'fore you're comin' back," Dad informed me as he swung his saddle from a limb to keep it out of porcupines' way.

Up into the treeless area of great jumbled rocks, steep treacherous slides, crumbling ledge and frozen banks of dirty snow we went, old Dad Lightfoot leading the way with that long, swinging stride of his. How that man can cover rough country! He's several years more than twice my age, but within an hour's time the pace he set had me practically exhausted.

I had hunted this country previously with a friend, and we had progressed over it only with great difficulty, being frequently forced to retrace our steps and detour. But with Dad leading the way it was different; there was never a false start, rarely even a false step. With uncanny judgment the old man selected the routes of advance, winding under cliffs, scrambling up over rocks, swinging across level spots— never halting, never pausing, always upward.

It was magnificent country, this stronghold of the mountain goat—rough, rugged, harsh and unbelievably huge. Great fingers and pinnacles and upthrusts of granite flung themselves at the blue sky. Deep crevices, cañons and ravines gouged the face of the mountain; snowbanks snuggled beneath the north faces of overhanging cliffs. Treacherous shale-rock slides sloped away in innocent-looking toboggans of death.

Dad and I were like two tiny, insignificant insects crawling laboriously over the footstool of the gods. But still, owning in our own minds all the world that we could see about us and gloriously indifferent to our insignificance, we pushed on. And always Dad had his eyes peeled for a flash of white or a little imprint in the thin soil. I stumbled along behind, content that he should do the sleuthing and concentrating my powers on staying with him.

High up under the peak, Dad dropped to his knees and pointed to a series of little heart-shaped tracks in the dust. A herd of goats had passed that way not long before.

"Got steel jackets in yore gun?" he asked in a whisper.

Mountain goats are thought to have adapted to steep alpine terrain to avoid predators such as wolves, bears, and cougars. This billy lives in the rugged terrain of Idaho's mountains. (Photograph © Erwin and Peggy Bauer)

I nodded. Normally I refuse to use metal-jacketed ammunition for big game, but this was a special occasion.

"Come on, then, an' don't make no racket."

Wriggling on his stomach like a lizard, the old man moved forward over loose shale. Imitating his movements, I followed, thinking that there was little need for all this extreme caution, since the crest of the ridge was still a hundred yards away, and I doubted if there was anything on the other side of it anyhow. But when my rifle barrel carelessly clinked against a stone, he turned and gave me a fierce stare. A second later his boots were sliding forward again.

Twenty minutes passed before Dad, having carefully removed his hat, raised himself slowly, inch by inch, until he could see over the slight rise. Then he crooked a gnarled finger, inviting me forward.

I covered the few feet at a snail's pace and managed to arrive without any undue noise. Then I too, inch by inch, raised myself until, with hardly any more than my eyebrows showing, I could see over the ridge and into the little swale beyond. A gentle puff of wind in my face told me that the old man had carefully and judiciously selected his avenue of approach.

I shall never forget the scene that met my eyes. At that moment I would have given the old mountaineer credit for wizardry. It was a feat that I had tried many times—and always failed.

Feeding on the scanty vegetation in that little swale, down through the center of which trickled the meltings of a glacier, were a score or more of shaggy white forms. It was a family gathering, billies, nannies and kids all being present. Some were lying down, some were feeding; the youngsters were frolicking. Two young males butted each other playfully, serving notice of what could be expected when they attained the age of rivalry for favor of the young nannies. With lowered head a watchful mother chased a young billy away from her kid.

The goats were ninety or a hundred yards from us, and to all outward appearances were entirely unaware of our presence. Dad had engineered a perfect stalk, and for one of the few times in a fairly wide hunting experience I was having the supreme pleasure of observing big game in its natural habitat, when its behavior was uninfluenced by fear of humans. I treasure those few minutes of recollection infinitely more than the mounted head which I secured on a previous hunt.

I could have watched them for hours, but a twitch at my pants leg reminded me that we had not come merely to observe. Little Benny was to be considered.

"Which one do you want?" I whispered.

"The big one, of course," he replied.

"Which big one?"

"The old grandpap—the big fellow on guard over by the rock pile."

Cautiously I raised myself again; I hadn't seen any goat on guard. But now I did, and what a goat! He was by far the biggest of the band. His hair was long and thick; the dark spikes of horns were unusually heavy. And he maintained an attitude of aloofness from the rest of the band. Truly an old patriarch!

My heart was pounding. Cautiously I pushed my rifle forward and lowered my head to the stock. The watchful old fellow must have caught a gleam of the barrel, because his ears came forward. I had my sights centered on his chest, just inside the foreleg, where I figured the metal-jacketed slug would do the most damage to the heart and the least to the hide.

Suddenly, Dad whispered in my ear. "Say, who's godfather here, anyhow?"

I turned my head to look at him. The expression in his eyes was suddenly covetous. Without a word, I pushed the rifle over to him.

Dad almost smacked his lips as he cuddled the stock to his old cheek. I saw his finger curl about the trigger. The steady squeezing of an expert rifle shot began. Then I turned my head to watch the goats.

It seemed a long time before the rifle spoke. At the report the scene before me erupted into violent action. White forms streaked for the protection of the rock maze, running with a peculiar choppy gallop. A young billy, in his frantic haste, attempted a sharp turn in some wet clay and landed heavily on

Billies and nannies are difficult to distinguish from each other, although female mountain goats are smaller in overall size and have more slender horns. (Photograph © Tom Tietz/The Green Agency)

Above: *Mountain goats live as low as sea level and as high as 10,000 or more feet. This goat lives in the mountains of Colorado.*
(Photograph © James Prout)
Overleaf: *This mountain goat overlooks Hidden Lake and the dramatic glacially sculpted landforms of Canada's Glacier National Park. (Photograph © Art Wolfe)*

his side, skidding to a halt. When he disappeared into the rocks, one side was plastered with yellow mud. A kid, deserted by its frightened mother, gazed about in wide-eyed wonder, trying to locate the source of that startling noise. Then, discovering that he was practically alone in the swale, he let out a dismayed bleat and ripped into an opening between two boulders.

But the old fellow on the higher rocks didn't run away. At the report of the rifle a shudder ran through his body. He made a single attempt to get to his feet, and then slowly settled back.

It is doubtful if the animal ever knew what struck him. Dad had placed his bullet with consummate skill. It entered the neck and smashed its way for a foot through the back-bone. Other than two small round holes the magnificent pelt didn't have a mark on it.

"Now there's a hide," old Dad Lightfoot said with deep satisfaction as he examined the carcass, "that little Benny can be proud of! Thank you, son, for comin' up an' gettin' it for me."

THE EDGES OF
AN ELK HUNT

by Dave Hughes

Dave Hughes, best known in the huge world of fly fishing, has authored over fifteen books. Among his other works, he has penned the instructional *Wet Flies: Tying and Fishing Soft-Hackles, Winged and Wingless Wets, and Fuzzy Nymphs* (1995), perhaps *the* most comprehensive guide on the subject; the informative *Deschutes: River of Renewal* (1990), a coffee table book covering the geology, history, boating, and fly fishing of the famous river; and the eloquent *Big Indian Creek* (1996), a week-long diary of a backpacking and fly fishing trip at a remote mountain stream in Oregon.

Hughes is a columnist for *Fly Rod & Reel* and *Fly Fishing and Tying Journal*, as well as a regular contributor to *Field & Stream* and other outdoors magazines. In the following story from the September 1998 issue of *Gray's Sporting Journal*, Hughes turns his talented pen to the world of big game, elucidating the beauty of the details surrounding an elk hunt in the Centennial Mountains.

B eauty often lies all around the edges of an elk hunt rather than at its center. What you remember when the hunt is over are the minor things you saw, or perhaps were never granted permission to see, rather than the elk you shot or did not.

A couple of seasons ago my brother Gene and I packed out of Lakeview Ranch into the Centennial Mountains somewhere on the border between Montana and Idaho. Gene's a doctor in Butte, Montana, and planned the hunt; he hinted that if I told you precisely where we went the resulting surgical procedure would be fun for him but not for me.

The pack in was pleasant, just eight or 10 miles up from the trail head on horses that rocked along gently, unmindful of all the gear we'd heaped upon them. Tony was our packer, a mountain man from Pennsylvania enthralled with being on a horse in country where the hillsides go up and up to knife-sliced ridges topped with snow. I got my first kick on the trip watching Tony get a kick out of where he was and what he was doing.

With base-camp tents already set up, Tony unpacked us and scolded his horses back down the trail, leaving Gene and I precisely what we wanted: no more than a drop camp at the edge of good game country.

The American elk is also called wapiti, which comes from a Shawnee word meaning "white rump." (Photograph © Stan Osolinski/The Green Agency)

Above: *This bull elk is in the rut, the annual period of sexual excitement when male deer break many of the rules—such as not standing in the middle of a meadow in broad daylight—of their ordinarily reclusive existence. (Photograph © Len Rue Jr.)*
Facing page: *Early European explorers wrote impressed accounts of the proud elk they found on the North American continent. (Photograph © Mark and Jennifer Miller Photos)*

We went in on Friday; the season opened Sunday morning, giving us Saturday to scout. It took a few hours to set up camp, and when we finally declared ourselves settled in, that last excellent hour of daylight remained. We hiked up the forested hill behind the tents until we found a clearing, then sat down and began glassing across a canyon to the far mountainside, which went up another 3,000 feet above the 7,000 or so where we sat.

The binoc's first quick scan swept through and was drawn back to three light dots a couple of miles up the canyon. These proved in the failing light to be a bachelor band of branched bulls.

"I picked good country," Gene said mildly when I got puffed up about being the one to spot them.

The next dawn we climbed back to the clearing above the tents and again spotted the bulls. We sat and plotted against them with the patience of hunt-

ers who have a full day in which they cannot hunt. Then we dropped back down to secure our camp while we spiked out. Because we were in bear country, Gene placed our food in a plastic bucket suspended in a tree. Let me say that we have spent a lot of time in bear country during which bears have remained only theoretical threats to our food supplies.

In early afternoon we hoisted our packs, slung our rifles and headed out of camp in opposite directions. Gene hiked a mile and a half up the continuation of the trail we'd ridden into camp and set his tiny tent below the island of timber and the park where we'd seen the elk. He planned to move up on the bulls in the morning, assuming they stayed where they were.

"Elk don't move out of a place like that unless they're disturbed," Gene had whispered, although we were still in base camp two miles from the elk.

I dropped into the canyon below camp, boulder-

hopped over a small stream and began zigzagging up the mountainside straight across from camp, digging footholds with my boots as I climbed past a V-notch in the Centennials through which the setting sun ignited the flat plains of Idaho 40 miles away.

At about 9,500 feet I found a ledge just wide enough for the tent, with just enough soil to grow grass and a few trees and not nearly as dangerous as I'm trying to keep from making it sound. I ate a cold dinner, although I had a stove and a hot dinner along, and watched masses of stars come out and drop so near that I might have reached up and swatted them.

When I awoke, the stars were hidden by mist that hung like a dropped ceiling across my ledge. I ate a cold breakfast in the cold dark and started across the face of the mountain as soon as enough light crept into the day. The ledge became a narrow cut clear across the mountainside, a trail that elk and deer used almost daily. I emerged from it onto a rounded ridgetop where I could look down across a series of ridges into the park where we'd seen the elk, a mile or so away.

It didn't take long, even in the low light and mist, to spot with binoculars a bull browsing a steep slope in the center of the park. I saw nothing of the other two but suspected their presence. I set up the spotting scope and was just beginning to estimate the bull's rack when the bull rolled a few feet down the slope and lay still in the grass—dead before I heard Gene's shot.

And this set into motion the second half of our plan. As soon as I saw Gene emerge from the timber and walk toward his animal, I jammed the scope into my day pack and began scrambling at right angles toward a ridgeline directly above the park, hoping to intercept the other bulls, at that moment still theories like the bear as they moved uphill in the draw.

I was half out of gas from the elevation and my hectic pace, still three ridgelines away from what I guessed would be the upward path of any elk moved out by Gene's shot, when a big mule deer buck jumped so near that it startled me as much as I startled it. It ran 200 yards up the ridge crest then stood broadside and peered at me, its after-half concealed behind a conifer and its chest exposed. I counted two points on each side through the scope and centered the cross hairs, weighing the near certainty of the forked horn against the uncertainty of the bull.

Indecision is at times a distinct decision. The buck bounded away into the mist before I could decide, and when I turned back to the ridgeline I saw elk—not just one or two but a herd—weaving in and out of scattered timber right where I'd expected them to be. They were still well below me but gaining ground toward the safety of the ceiling of mist and the other side of the mountain as fast as I was gaining ground on my sidehill gallop to intercept them. I goosed myself to greater speed and was soon across two more ridgelines and bending over for air.

When I edged over the last rounded ridge I saw an elk plodding slowly through a bemeadowed bowl, no more than a hundred feet from some stunted trees that would conceal and deliver it safely into the mist. My first thought was, I didn't get here in time. That's the last one at the tail end of the herd, and it's a cow.

But through the binoculars I saw horns disappearing into the mist, and when the elk turned I saw brow tines. I rested the rifle barrel over my hand on a tree limb, not estimating the range at the 250 to 300 yards it turned out to be but figuring I could hold the .300 Weatherby right where I wanted to hit so long as I left vital room below my aiming point.

At the shot the elk turned and continued to walk at the same speed but in the opposite direction. I shot twice more, and the bull rolled after the third shot but not in reaction to it. I found a single 180-grain Nosler Partition opened out perfectly beneath the skin on the far side of the bull's rib cage and found no sign of the second or third shot, which doesn't brag much about my shooting.

As I walked toward the downed bull, a milling herd of elk not 75 yards away stared wild-eyed at the beast appearing suddenly from the sharp roaring above them and bolted down the ridge, and I didn't need binoculars to see the massive, balanced rack on the six-point bull nearest me.

At four years, a bull usually has the mature six-tine antlers that appear on this Rocky Mountain elk. (Photograph © Stan Osolinski/The Green Agency)

* * *

Draw back for a moment now, and gaze across this great Montana hillside from your omniscient reader's viewpoint. You'll see the mountaintop cut off levelly by white mist and a series of grassy ridges with scattered trees probing down out of the mist toward heavy timber. You'll see a white dot that is me stripped down to a T-shirt even in the cold, slowly gutting and skinning a five-point elk in a meadow just beneath the line drawn across the mountain by the mist. A mile straight down the hill you'll see Gene doing the same thing with the patience of someone with an entire day ahead in which to do it.

If you listen with me for a moment while I work, you'll hear the unseasonal bugling of a bull elk high up in the mist above—bugling that sounds like some mythical Elk of Elks up there in the clouds lamenting the loss of a little brother. I know nothing of elk emotions nor do I know why he was bugling, but it sounded like that to me, and at the same time it somehow compelled me to come back. I can't explain this, just as I can't explain a lot of things about elk hunting.

When my elk was emptied and skinned I propped it open to the cold air, tagged it and hiked back over the ridges and along the cut to gather my spike camp, eating old snow all the way because I was long out of water and far above any springs or streams.

I found Gene not long before dark, just hanging the last quarter of his elk in a tree at the edge of the timber. He said a herd of elk with a six-point bull had run past while he was dressing his bull. I said it probably was the same herd I'd seen. He said he'd seen his herd before I shot, which meant two herds of elk were running around up there with bulls, in addition to the Elk of Elks I'd heard on the mountain above.

We hatched a plot to get the two elk off the mountain, which involved my staying in Gene's spike camp below the timber, his hiking into base camp on the horse trail by flashlight, then my moving back to base camp in the morning while he hiked out to get Tony and his horses to carry out the elk quarters. If it sounds complicated it's because Gene's not just a doctor but a colonel, and his plans are quickly amended if the average person can understand them. It worked out exactly the way he planned, which is almost always what happens.

Gene's spike camp was nestled in trees alongside a small trout lake that I marked down as a place I'd like to return to in summer. I built a small fire, cooked and ate Gene's dinner and slept well.

I had just hiked into base camp the next morning and was preparing to enjoy a long rest when Gene and Tony rode in all fresh and ready to go get elk. We went after mine first because it was almost straight up from Gene's, but under my guidance we went one ridge too far and wound up facing a sharp canyon the horses could not cross. As the day had gotten long Tony wisely decided to back out, pick up Gene's elk on the way to base camp and return for mine the next day.

With the four quarters of Gene's elk on the horses, I suddenly decided I had no good reason to go with them. My spike camp was still packed; I still had the uncooked dinner from the first night and could melt snow for water. I shouldered my pack and headed up as Gene and Tony mounted their horses and rode down.

I worked my way up to the meadow in the fading light and set my tent a hundred feet or so from the elk. Because the temperature had never gone above 40 here and the elk had been skinned, it would keep fine another day.

Part of a moon rose, and by its slim light I began to gather snow in my cook pot. The deepest snow lay under trees that blocked the light, and for some reason I worked up grizzly bear visions in the darkness. I can't say that I scared myself much, but I didn't stop looking over my shoulder until I got back to the open meadow and the faint moonlight.

When I touched a match to the stove a flame jetted out a foot in the wrong direction, and when I examined the stove by headlamp I discovered the fuel line had quarreled with the spotting scope in my day pack and lost.

I went back into the grizzly bear woods, gathered twigs and branches and started a small fire on a gravel stream bed. It takes a long time to melt enough snow for a man dehydrated by exertion and high altitude to drink and to cook a freeze-dried meal, but I had no reason to hurry, and that night in the meadow just below 10,000 feet, with my elk chilled out nearby and the grizzly bears of my imaginings prowling around in the nearby woods, became one of that hunt's most pleasant memories.

This silhouette shows off the majestic upsweep and branching tines of trophy elk antlers. (Photograph © Dušan Smetana)

When I had a water bottle full for the next day, I boiled a cup of melted snow, sprinkled in a packet of chocolate mix, poured in a shot of Black Velvet from a miniature flask and sat cross-legged beneath the slice of moon and the stars in the beauty of the meadow, sipping.

In the morning a heavy mist again lay over the mountain, animated now by wind. Every tree and shrub and blade of grass hung heavy with frost, and in the morning light the mountainside was beautiful and ghostlike.

I loaded my rifle and hunted for a short time along the underside of the mist, telling myself I was looking for that forked horn I'd let go earlier, though I knew I was not. I just wanted to be up there in what seemed like some strange room frozen in time, with the ceiling of doom hanging down close enough that I could throw my hat and hit it.

Later in the morning I found an easy route down and met Tony and Gene on their way up with the pack horses and with news that not all bears are dreams or theories.

"The smartest bear in Montana came into our camp while we were out," Gene said. "It ate everything in the bucket, ripped open the tent and tore up my down bag, and it carried off the pants I was wearing when I got my elk."

"Grizzly bear or black?" I asked.

"There's no grizzlies around here."

I kept quiet about that. "Why smart?" I said.

"It took the pants that had my wallet with the bear tag in it."

"Smart bear," I agreed.

We quartered my elk and loaded it onto the horses; Gene and Tony would ride to base camp, get Gene's elk and head out to hang it beyond the reach of bears. With my riding horse converted to a pack horse, I would have to hike back to camp, which in truth I preferred.

"If you get time, look around for my pants," Gene said. "And if you see that bear, shoot it."

Elk are one of the largest members of the deer family, second in size only to the moose. (Photograph © D. Robert Franz)

"I don't have a bear tag," I said.

"If you kill it I'll pay the fine." I'm not sure if he was joking, but as I never saw the bear I didn't have to find out.

I did see what the bear had done. Food wrappings were scattered through trees for a hundred yards. The sleeping tent was ripped open and looked as though kids had enjoyed a pillow fight inside. I rested awhile and ate a hot lunch then began to walk around the tent in tight concentric circles. Two hours, 75 yards and 10 orbits later I found Gene's wool pants bitten full of holes and lying on a patch of snow. The bear failed its IQ test: It left the tag.

Gene rode back in the next day with his son Graham; they led another horse for me. Above us the wind-driven mists slowly huffed up a blizzard. Angry clouds rose over the mountain from the north, and when the sun slanting in from the southwest hit the first flakes of snow it lit them like sparks.

The next morning we saddled up and rode far up the trail. As we climbed, the timber opened out and alternated with open parks. It looked like great elk country, but the wind drove the snow so hard that we could seldom see beyond our three horses tramping along slowly with their heads down.

Because it was Graham's first day in and he was full of stories we'd told him of elk running around all over the place, we made a couple of short hunts in half-circles so he could get some energy off and feel like he had a chance at getting one. Those elk were hunkered in that timber somewhere, driven into it by our harassment and still deeper by the blizzard. It became our agreement that the smartest thing to do was to get under some trees and light a big fire.

And that became another peripheral memory of the hunt: sitting on a log and talking with Gene and Graham, surrounded by all the good elk country that we could not see, pushing wood into the fire and watching it blaze up quickly into the swirling snow. By the time we rode back into base camp late that afternoon, the snow was half a foot deep and not letting up.

The storm blew itself out sometime in the night. In the morning the sun was out and the big sky deep blue above a mountainous landscape bright white beneath a foot of soft snow.

Gene prescribed himself a day off in camp, satisfied to have an elk hanging. Graham picked up the

Above: *September is the month of bugling, as bull elk like this one attempt to gather harems of does and protect them against other rutting bulls. (Photograph © Dušan Smetana)*
Facing page: *Elk bone and antler have been found in some of the oldest human-inhabited sites in North America. (Photograph © Daniel J. Cox/Natural Exposures Inc.)*

tracks of the marauding bear not far from camp—it had come sniffing back—and tracked it for miles through the snow without ever catching sight of it, though he was sure he had come close. I assigned myself a different kind of day off.

I decided to gain some elevation with my horse, then leave it and side-hill across ridges one canyon up from the one where I'd shot my elk. I'd look into some new country, take my time, glass for game and enjoy all that beauty laid out below me. I didn't want to go far and didn't.

At midmorning I tied the horse in a copse of trees and shuffled slowly through snow over the first ridge, working through a shallow draw then over the next ridge. As I began to traverse the ridge, a smallish four-point mule deer emerged in a shower of snow from a round island of stunted trees and headed down toward denser timber in lazy butts-up bounds.

The buck was little more than a hundred yards

away, quartering. I swung the rifle and touched it off when the cross hairs passed its rib cage. The buck didn't react so I shot once more—not really necessary but not really a mistake. The first shot had been almost surgical; the second shot ruined some meat and put the buck down at once.

The memory of that buck bounding out of the trees and down through the clean snow after such a short and easy hunt through all that high beauty remains as vivid as the day the hunt ended in the elk itself.

The next day brought another snapshot frozen in time and memory. Graham and I still-hunted through the snow on a timbered ridgeline above camp, slipping along for a couple of hours without seeing any signs of elk, our view restricted by timber and rarely exceeding 30 yards. Graham, spent from the much more exciting work of chasing the bear all

Above: *This bull sports the reddish-brown coat and orange-colored rump of elk in the summer. (Photograph © Thomas D. Mangelsen/ Images of Nature)*
Overleaf: *A bull elk bedded at Gibbon Meadow in Yellowstone National Park. (Photograph © Doug Locke)*

the previous day, reacted with only mild interest when I pointed out that we were suddenly in the midst of a complication of meandering elk tracks in the new snow.

I was trying to whisper to Graham that something might happen at any moment when the timber exploded and a file of elk thrashed across our bow. I expected a bull to be last and told Graham to get ready. He was fumbling to get his thick gloves off and still had his rifle slung over his shoulder when the last and largest of the elk came into sight from the right, passed in front of us for some seconds at shotgun range, then disappeared to our left.

It was a big old cow. I think Graham recognized how he'd have felt had it been a bull. We hunted out the day with heightened interest and colder hands but saw no more elk.

The next and final day Graham and I hunted the high ridges coming off the mountain across from camp while Gene rode up the canyon hoping for a buck to end his hunt. Graham and I climbed and glassed, and we jumped a herd of deer that should have had a small buck among them but didn't. We glassed a lone, large deer higher up in some scrub brush that should have been a buck and might have been. It was far enough away that binoculars could miss horns but not large ones. I watched it for a long time, trying to make a buck out of it, before it disappeared into some stunted trees.

We turned away and hiked toward a ridgetop covered in snow, and here is where I had my last retained vision of the hunt.

On top of the ridge, above us, backlit and out in the open, no more than a hundred yards away, a bull elk stood broadside, embodying all the majesty that elk alone on this continent seem to have. It had seen us, and it held its head high and turned it from side to side, as though to better understand us.

Finally it turned and bolted. I looked at Graham, his rifle to his shoulder and prepared to fire, but then he lowered it: The elk was a big old bull, for some reason either still a spike or reverted to one in its old age. It was all well done by Graham, for only bulls with branched antlers were legal where we hunted.

"I'd have got it," Graham said, and I remembered the fire in him. He was as excited simply by seeing that elk and being ready for it as he would have been had he made it his.